"I learned a lot of new and useful ideas, which continue to help me to this day. I definitely recommend her workshop for new teachers, but even veteran teachers will benefit."

J. BONEAU
Drama Teacher

"All the ideas that I have acquired from the Classroom Management program work in making my classroom function smoothly. The duty and responsibility sheet has made a huge difference in managing the class and getting all students involved."

E. BOYD
Spanish Teacher

"Prior to 2010, I practiced Dental Hygiene for twenty years. I decided to pursue my lifelong dream to become a teacher. Mentors and fellow teachers would tell me I needed to improve my classroom management skills, but no one told me how to do it. I read books and got on the internet, but nothing helped. I taught for 2 years and went back to Dental Hygiene for 1 year. I was exhausted and felt like a failure as a teacher. After sharing my concerns, Regina walked me through her Classroom Management program and it has totally changed my life. I have implemented the program and I am here to tell you, 'it works'. Not only does it keep my students behaving as they should, it has made my life easier. I am working 'smarter not harder'. I now love my job and enjoy being a teacher like I always dreamed".

R. MORALES
Health Science Teacher

Classroom Management

A Step-By-Step Comprehensive Approach

Regina McClinton Jackson

Regina McClinton Jackson
© 2011 Revised 2016

All right reserved. No part of the publication may be reproduced or transmitted in any form, including photocopy, recording, or any information storage and retrieval system without permission in writing from the publisher. Printed in the United States of America

Design cover by Regina M. Jackson sponsored by previous Classroom Management by RMJ participants and illustrations from https://pixabay.com

ISBN: 978-0-9898997-2-7 (sc)
ISBN: 978-0-9898997-3-4 (spiral-bound)
ISBN: 978-0-9898997-4-1 (ebk)

Published by
Jackson Services
www.jacksonservices.biz

<u>Dedication</u>

Dedicated to my husband, Elijah Jackson, a retired teacher after thirty years of service.

Acknowledgements

Special appreciation to Diane Franz, Irene Howard, Calvin Payne, and Samuel Thompson.

Thank you to Sherrie Clark and Storehouse Publishing, LLC for all of their efforts in putting the final polishing touches on this book and seamlessly taking care of those specialized issues that were needed before going to print.

Preface

As an educator for over twenty years, I have experienced many classroom issues. As I journey toward the end of my career as a classroom teacher, I thought it would be beneficial to put some of my experiences to print. As a teacher, I was inspired to get a Master of Art in Teaching, and one of the courses I took was classroom management.

As a course requirement, I had to write papers each week presenting challenges I faced in the classroom and how I addressed them. I put together a few of the papers and the documents I developed during my teaching career, and I am sharing them with you.

In this book, I provide the rational for why I created each document.

I learned three very important lessons over the course of my years as a classroom teacher:

1. Documentation,
2. Documentation, and
3. Documentation.

I think you get the point.

Table of Contents

Chapter 1: Personal System of Discipline and Classroom Procedures 1

Chapter 2: Literature Review 7

Chapter 3: Managing Students with Conduct Issues_My Personal System of Discipline 9

Chapter 4: Technology and Collaboration 13

Chapter 5: Become a Facilitator 15

Chapter 6: How to Get Students Off to a Great Start_the First Four Days of School 17

Chapter 7: Rational Behind the Various Logs and_Sheets Developed 21

References 33

Forms 35

Chapter One

Personal System of Discipline and Classroom Procedures

Imagine a situation where all students quietly enter the classroom and are sitting in their seats before the tardy bell rings. All students put nonessential items under their workstation and only have the material that pertains to the course out. All students turn in their assignment within one or two minutes after the tardy bell rings.

This is the procedure that I use for my health science classes at DeBakey High School for Health Professions. This procedure would be ideal if all students followed the rules for entering class as well as turning in all assignments and staying on task. The students that usually enter the classroom noisily are often the same students who are not on task and do not turn in their assignments on time. This is only about five percent of the students in my class, but that five percent can disrupt the entire class.

The procedure in place for students who violate my classroom conduct rules includes the student signing the student conduct log. This procedure will be discussed later in the book.

My goal is somewhat aggressive, but I would like to reach those five percent of the students and have one hundred percent of my students on task with positive behavior.

Each teacher should have his or her own system of discipline that works well for his for her classroom. I have a system that works well for me. Because my students are training for careers in health science, I operate my class like a business. I am more of a facilitator (CEO of Jackson's Class) than a teacher. The sign on my door makes students aware of this.

I try to instill in my students that being punctual to work or school is very important. I explain that in many healthcare professions, employees cannot leave their job unless relieved by an employee from the incoming shift. Therefore, it is critical for employees to report to work on time.

To help train my students to be punctual, all of my students must be sitting in their assigned seats before the tardy bell rings. Students put all nonessential items under their work station or in a cubby and only have the materials that pertain to the course on their work station.

A typical day begins and/or ends with students turning in assignments by placing the assignment in their assigned mailbox slot within one or two minutes of the beginning or ending bells for class.

After I welcome my students each day, I call my class supervisor forward to begin the class by reading a script which is located on the outside of my supervisor log book (RMJ 20). The class supervisor leads the class in roll call and brings the log book to me to verify and post attendance in the computer. Part of the script read by the class supervisor asks all students to check their area for any trash left behind by the previous class. Any trash is reported to the supervisor using the appropriate log sheet (RMJ 23).

After the supervisor is finished, which usually takes about two minutes, the assistant class supervisors #1 and #2 are called forward. The assistant supervisors also read from a script that is posted on the wall by the assignment calendar (RMJ 21). Assistant supervisor #1 reads the daily assignment listed from the calendar as the class follows along on their daily assignment calendar provided at the beginning of school.

The assistant supervisor #1 also reads what will take place next class period as the students highlight the assignments on their copy. While assistant supervisor #1 is reading the calendar, assistant supervisor # 2 is checking the basket for handouts and announcements. When assistant supervisor # 1 is finished, attention is given to assistant supervisor #2 to read his or her part of the script (RMJ 21) that I have posted on the wall by the student baskets.

If announcements are in the basket, assistant supervisor # 2 will read them to the class. Some announcements are read directly from my computer. Oftentimes the counselors will email or send information concerning great opportunities for students.

I have the assistant supervisor summarize the information to the class, and I forward the information to any interested students. I do not print the information sent by email. There is a sheet in the student basket that reads, "Please read announcements from computer."

When it is facing up, the assistant supervisor knows there is an announcement to read. When it is facing down, the assistant supervisor knows that there are no computer announcements. The assistant supervisor # 2 also checks the basket for handouts.

If there is a stack of handouts, then the assistant supervisor will call up the teacher assistants to pass out any papers that need to be issued to the students. After this is done, students summarize health-related current events articles for a grade or extra credit.

Health-related current events are mandatory every other cycle. Having students research current events articles and summarize their findings to their peers is training for careers in corporate America.

Articles were also posted on *Edmodo®*, (discussed in the technology chapter), for all students to view so as to prevent duplication of articles. To ensure that students are focused and know exactly what to do each day, students always have an ongoing assignment to do the first fifteen to twenty minutes of class. These are the daily classroom procedures that take place in all of my health-science classes at DeBakey High School for Health Professions. The daily process takes about seven to ten minutes each day.

In addition to the class supervisor, assistant supervisor, and teacher assistants doing their daily jobs, other students are called upon to do class duties and are assigned. Therefore, all students have a job assignment in my classes (See RMJ 18).

As stated earlier, the class is a job training course, so the class has a more business-like structure than a traditional classroom. I am more of a facilitator than a teacher. I keep all of my students busy and focused, so I have very few discipline problems. My class runs very smoothly on a daily basis for the most part, but a few students will still break rules.

My personal discipline system for my students is to discuss the rules for how students should conduct themselves in class at the beginning of each year along with the consequences. Students know how their conduct grade will be determined.

I have parents and students sign a form stating that the grading policy was read and understood. The form is kept on file. Each time a student breaks a conduct rule, the student must sign the appropriate log sheet (see RMJ 9). After four conduct violations, the student will receive an "S" in conduct, and parents are notified that if one more conduct violation occurs (five), the students will receive a "P" in conduct.

After five or more conduct violations, the student will be sent to the office for discipline. Punishment ent may include a parent conference, detention, an office "P" or "U," probation and review for exit.

I do have a system in place for students to restore their conduct, so students can learn from their mistakes and not be sent to the office. To rectify the behavior, students are allowed to write twenty-five positive sentences concerning their conduct violation so that they can have their good conduct record restored. By allowing students to redeem their conduct, I allow students to have a cooperative stake in their conduct grade. In addition to the above restorative options, students must do either a lunchtime or afterschool detention to restore their conduct from a "P" to an "S." Students are never allowed to go from a "P" to an "E."

Because I am training students to conduct themselves in a professional workplace setting, students receive a professionalism grade that accounts for ten percent of their cycle grade.

During their eleventh and twelfth grade years, our students do group rotations through various hospitals as part of the Health Science course curriculum. Students are told that in real-life job situations, employees are evaluated on performance and professionalism.

Excellent evaluations on a job usually result in monetary awards, promotions, and increase in pay or rank. However, poor evaluations may result in an employee getting fired. Students are told that rules must be followed in order to prevent losing points from their professionalism grade.

Students begin each cycle or week with one hundred points. Ten points are taken off each time a student violates one of the professionalism rules. The professional grade is tracked by the professionalism log (RMJ 10 and RMJ 10a). Students are allowed to write twenty-five positive sentences concerning their professionalism violation in order to have their points restored.

Students receive their professional grade every week in the form of a professionalism grade paycheck (see RMJ 10b). Bonus points are given to students who return their check the next class period.

To encourage students to be timely when returning parent signature documents, no points are given for late checks. It is optional that students take the paychecks home for parent signatures. The only time parent signatures are required is when I must communicate information to parents who do not have an email address on file. If the student paycheck is not returned after two class periods, then failure to return the document becomes a conduct violation.

The professionalism paycheck is a unique way for me to give my students their professionalism grade and communicate to parents. Most students get parent signatures, which allow them to earn bonus points.

I do poll parents to make sure they are the ones actually signing the check and not their student. I only send checks home weekly for my juniors because they are more grade-conscious than other grade levels. The weekly paycheck process did not work well for my freshman, so I only send checks home when needed.

As a facilitator, I run my class more like a boss than like a teacher. My personal system of discipline involves keeping my students organized and on task. Students know what I expect, and my standards are high. I always follow through on any disciplinary issues according to my grading policy. (See sample grading policy).

I document each disciplinary infraction for use during parent conferences. In my many years of teaching, I have had very few parent conferences because of student behavior. I am seldom challenged by students or parents about numeric or conduct grades due to the fact that I have clear policies signed by students and parents, and I document each infraction. This system works for me and can work for other teachers.

There were several systems of discipline I explored when I was pursuing my Master of Arts in Teaching (MAT). I did a comparison and contrast to my system of discipline. After considering several techniques, I considered Barbara Coloroso's Inner Discipline System® to be an effective one. In regards to students, Coloroso states to give students the opportunity to make decisions, take responsibility for their actions, and learn from their successes and mistakes (Charles, 2005, p. 147).

As stated previously, I try to have students learn from their mistakes by writing twenty-five positive sentences pertaining to the conduct violation in order to have their conduct restored. If the student makes the same mistake twice, the students must write fifty sentences. Each time the students make the same mistake, the sentences increase by twenty-five.

For example, if students talk too much or too loud three times, they must write seventy-five sentences to get their conduct restored. The students will write, "I will speak softly during class."

My concept is for students to learn from their mistakes by writing positive sentences to reinforce positive behavior. Since I have started the process of letting students learn from their mistakes, I have not had to send any students to the office.

Students make the decision to write the sentences, and/or serve detention or keep the conduct cut. Most students make the decision to write the sentences and serve detention. My goal is to add something extra and more rewarding for the students to get enriched from their mistakes.

Another discipline technique I have found to be effective is Linda Albert's Cooperative Discipline System®. Albert's focus is what she calls the three C's—capable, connect, and contribute. The teacher helps the student feel that he or she is able to accomplish any task with or without the help of others and encourages the student to apply themselves academically.

The teacher should also have a system in place to make students feel connected to the teacher as well as to the other students in the class in a positive manner. I have all of my junior medical lab students serve the role as "teacher for a day" and teach a lab. In large classes, students have a partner and co-teach. This positive relationship promotes positive behavior.

When it comes to conduct issues, all students should have an opportunity to make a contribution to the class; therefore, teachers should work cooperatively with students to develop a set of consequences that the students feel is reasonable. With this process, students will most likely abide by the rules and accept the consequences without rebellion. The consequences that I currently have in place were developed over a period of years and were based on a trial-and-error process of previous students in my class wanting a way to restore their conduct grade when they violated a conduct rule (Charles, 2005, p. 200-201).

Coloroso's and Albert's focuses tie together with my current classroom procedures in that I can apply both of their principles using my classroom behavior management procedures. Students learn from their mistakes and cooperatively accept the consequences set in place.

Finding a way to encourage students to stay on task is another issue that many teachers face, including me. There are many techniques that teachers can use. One of these techniques include an interactive game that students can play daily that rewards good behavior and penalizes behavior that violates classroom rules.

One creative game is based on monopoly. The theme for the Monopoly board game is called "We are on the right track Monopoly game." In the game, when students stay on track, they advance forward through the Monopoly board game. When students get off tack, they go to jail. To get out of jail and back into the game, the students must do something positive. There is a reward for students who get to the finish line (Classroom Management).

I have a similar system in place based on a game that rewards all students as a class if all students are on task; no student is late to class; all students turn in assignments; and no students sign the conduct log. If these criteria are met, then all students get five extra credit points applied toward their major grade category.

I explain to my students that I am using "real world" practices by rewarding the group when all members of a team work together. In corporate America when productivity is high, and the company has a substantial increase in profits, employees typically receive bonuses or other rewards. So, I too give a bonus when all students are on task.

Because no single student wants to be the cause of the class not receiving extra credit points, this method encourages class cooperation and compliance. This method also encourages students to help each other and warn each other when they observe negative behavior.

This system works great, but in addition to giving daily bonus points when the whole class is on task, my future plans are to give each student a personal Monopoly board game. Each day the student is on task, he or she will advance one space on the Monopoly board.

If a student gets off task, the student will go to jail, and the only way to get out of jail is to (a) turn in the missing assignment, (b) write conduct sentences pertaining to the conduct violation, or (c) make a positive presentation to the class. For example, give a presentation reviewing a health-related current event article to the class when it is not mandatory. When the student gets to the finish line, he/she will be rewarded with extra-credit points added to the major test category. This approach will allow the students to be rewarded individually and collectively.

Having classroom procedures in place to discourage negative and disruptive behavior is essential in order for teachers to meet the many demands set forth by local school districts and the state and federal governing agencies. When teachers have such a system in place, classroom time becomes more productive and students better understand the relationship between positive behavior and effective work ethic.

Chapter Two

Literature Review

One of the most critical components of education is having a managed classroom environment in which students can learn. If a classroom environment is not well-managed, effective learning cannot be taking place. If effective student learning is not taking place in the classroom, the educational system is robbing students of the best possible education.

Many books, magazines, and articles have been published that present solutions for effective classroom management. I reviewed four such articles and examined the feasibility of each in different classroom settings and in my particular classroom.

Article 1: What is your classroom management profile?

This was a very interesting article in which teachers can learn about different individual management styles. Teachers can take a survey of questions to see which management profile they fit into. The four styles are authoritarian, authoritative, laissez-faire, and indifferent.

The teacher that fits into authoritarian style of management places firm limits and controls on the students. Students will often be in their assigned seats, will be quiet, be seated before the tardy bell, and have desks positioned in straight rows. Students do not interrupt the teacher, and verbal exchanges and discussion are discouraged.

The authoritarian's students do not have the opportunity to learn and/or practice communication skills. The authoritarian prefers vigorous discipline and expects students to follow and obey directions, or students will be disciplined according to the class rules.

Authoritative teachers place limits and controls on the students but simultaneously encourage independence. If a student is disruptive, the teacher offers a polite but firm reprimand. The authoritative teacher does allow considerable verbal interaction, even critical debates, but students usually are not given the opportunity to expand their communication skills.

The laissez-faire teacher will place few demands or controls on the students in the classroom. "Do your own thing" describes this classroom environment. The laissez-faire teacher accepts the students' impulses and actions and is less likely to monitor their behaviors.

The indifferent teacher does not care about the classroom environment and is not involved in the classroom management process. This teacher places few demands, if any, on the students and appears generally uninterested.

According to the survey, my highest score was for the authoritarian style of teaching, followed by authoritative style of managing. I have very low scores for the laissez-faire and indifferent style of teaching.

I do agree with the survey, but I see myself as more of an authoritative teacher. I do allow quite a bit of verbal interaction, and my students have the opportunity to learn and practice communication skills. However, I do not encourage debates between students and myself. (Teacher Talk, Volume 1, Issue 2: What is your classroom management profile? Last Updated: December 4)

Article 2: Classroom Management Monopoly

This article on classroom management deals with the trend of managing the classroom by encouraging students to stay on task. Students who are on task are the least likely to misbehave.

Students play a daily game like Monopoly. In this game when students stay on track, they advance forward through the Monopoly board game.

When students get off track, they go to jail on the board. To get out of jail, students must do something positive to get back in the game. There is a reward for students who get to the finish line.

I agree with this concept of classroom management and believe it can work great in any classroom environment (Pollan).

Article 3: Classroom Set-Up: Grades 3-12

This article discusses the typical classrooms and gives suggestions for a different type of classroom setup to promote better classroom management.

The article suggests that teachers should stray away from the rows or groups of three to four tables. It states that studies show that the further back you go in the rows, the more discipline problems occur because visual and physical stimulation from the teacher is increasingly diminished.

The suggestion is to arrange the chairs/tables into a three-sided "box" shape (|_|). In this fashion, EVERY STUDENT IS IN THE FIRST ROW!

With this setup, teachers can freely move around the room while talking and therefore giving "personal" contact with each student. The result will be greater attention from the students and fewer discipline problems.

I do agree with this classroom management style. I switched classrooms with another teacher, and her classroom was designed in the "box" shape. The students in that class were always quiet and on task, more than the students that were in my lab class where students sit in groups of four at tables.

It never occurred to me that the reason students behaved better was because of the seating arrangement (Mandel).

Article 4: From Tourists to Citizens in the Classroom

This article discusses the effectiveness of a classroom constitution similar to the U.S. Constitution. The two elements for this system to be effective is consistency management and cooperative discipline, which is a program that builds citizenship in the classroom through experience.

The article compares teacher-centered classrooms vs. person-centered classrooms. I agree with this article, and experience has taught me that consistency management is a definite key to effective classroom management (Freiberg, 1996, pp. 32-36).

Each of the four articles discusses different aspects of classroom management and do not refute each other. Therefore, each has positive aspects that work with certain management styles.

It is important for a teacher to recognize his or her management style and try to improve it to meet the needs of his or her students. Any game or activity that will promote better behavior in students, while allowing for a constructive learning environment, is an excellent classroom management technique. The arrangement of the classroom seats can also be a key factor in classroom management. However, when it is all said and done, consistency in the application of classroom procedure and student expectations are key to effective classroom management.

Chapter Three
Managing Students with Conduct Issues
My Personal System of Discipline

When most teachers attend a classroom management workshop or read a book, they are searching for the magic potion or top-secret answer to make all students have good behavior. The truth is, there is no single approach to attain good student behavior. Teachers should find what works best for their school environment as well as their individual class environment.

I found what works best for me is just documenting bad behavior and having consequences in place for negative behavior as well as rewarding good behavior. In this chapter, I will share my personal experiences that have worked best for me during my span as a classroom teacher of over twenty years.

Each year, teachers across the nation issue a set of conduct rules for students to follow throughout the school year. The problem is, the rules that are issued at the beginning of the year are protocolled by the school or school district. Students know it is protocol and that teachers are following procedure.

The story explained within this book are of my trials as a first-year teacher and how I was challenged by students each time a rule was broken. Years of experience have taught me that when students know they are being documented, and students sign off on it, it tends to diminish the behavioral issues.

When the time comes for a teacher to send a student to the office, call a parent, or even have a parent conference after a set number of conduct issues, the process becomes a breeze because the pattern of bad behavior is documented. In my class, students are rarely sent to the office or have student/parent conferences due to the policies and procedures in place.

When a student breaks a rule, many teachers do not want to approach students or want to have a confrontation with a student, especially in front of the class. That is why the way the teacher approaches students is just as important as documenting the event.

Teachers must approach students with respect and speak in a soft and calm tone of voice. When students are spoken to in a rude and disrespectful tone, most students will retaliate in the same manner. That's when a confrontation can occur between a teacher and student.

It is important to nicely explain to the student why he or she is signing the log book and the continued consequences. Giving a "real world" example of a similar type of the behavior in the workplace helps the student relate his or her behavior to an outside experience to clearly understand the importance of documenting the behavioral issue. Naturally, students don't like it, but most students sign the log books with a humble and regretful attitude for their behavior.

Students have a process in place for restoring his or her conduct if the student wishes to do so. As discussed previously, students have a grace period of two to three weeks before signing the temporary or permanent conduct logs. During this grace period, students are constantly reminded that when the grace period is over, the process of documentation of students breaking rules will begin.

However, some students don't break their first rule during the grace period and have to sign the log book halfway through the school year for their first offense. It is never a good feeling to have a student sign, but having the ethics to be fair and equal to all of my students concerning my rules encourages me to do so.

Just recently I thought of putting a roster on the wall or log book. Each time the student breaks a rule, he or she will get a strike by his or her name. After students receive three strikes, he or she will start signing the permanent log book. I would use this process in place of the three-week grace period, which will allow each student to have his or her very own grace period.

I ran the process by my students at the end of this current school year, and the students thought it was a great idea and wish I had done it for them. With this method, I won't feel bad when any student has to sign the log book for any reason because he or she had three personal warnings.

The other procedure I have in place before having students sign the conduct log is to give a grading policy quiz during the first or second week of school. In my early days, students had to pass the quiz or write the policy five times for a grade of 100 that would help boost their failing grade, or students could retake a different policy quiz until he or she received a passing grade. Nowadays, students take the policy quiz and receive the grade for the first attempt at the quiz. With many versions of the policy quiz, students are threatened with the fact that a pop quiz can be given at any time if the class gets too loud or out of control.

Teachers must also remember to be a fair and equal-opportunity disciplinarian. Students quickly recognize teachers who are selective disciplinarians. If a student is popular or well-liked, then the student may have a tendency to escape discipline.

Striving hard to be equal and fair to all students is not an easy task. It breaks my heart to have my sweet, quiet student, my smart student, or my student who is even nice and friendly to me sign the log when he or she breaks the rules, but I do. Even sweet, quiet, and nice students break rules. These are the same students who turn out to be rule breakers in life because he or she had escaped discipline all through their education experience. They assume the rules don't apply to them.

Students are very observant and take notice of teachers who pick which students to discipline. This fact was reported by former students. Adopting the aforementioned process for the individual grace period could help teachers make every effort to be a fair disciplinarian to all students.

As a classroom teacher, one must decide upfront that his or her discipline reputation will be known not only among the students but among the other teachers and administrators. Some teachers want to have a reputation of being nice, well–liked, or even friends and on the same level as their students. Some teachers, like me, have a reputation among students as being strict.

Personally, I don't mind having a reputation of being strict. Many students who take my course know of my no-nonsense policy before they're presented with a set of rules.

Am I well-liked by the majority of students? No, but that is not my mission as a career and technology teacher. However, many students respect my classroom discipline and inform me of that fact when returning for a visit.

Keep in mind that my classroom is ran like a business, with my acting as the CEO. The students are informed at the beginning of each school year or new rotation that I will be a tough boss, but I will most likely not be toughest boss they will encounter on a job. The students are acting as my employees, and each student has an assigned job.

Constantly put in the forefront of each student's mind is that the end goal of his or her educational experiences is to obtain and maintain a job due to positive behavior and a strong work ethic. Students are also told upfront that he or she will be disciplined out of love, just like parents discipline out of love, with the intentions of his or her offspring becoming the best person they can be in life.

Furthermore, students are told that the policies and procedures are in place so they can be the best person he or she can be in the workplace as well as in life.

In addition to being a fair disciplinarian, another way of cutting down on negative behavior is to always keep students on task. When students know what to do and always have an assignment pending, this allows the students to feel the urgency to not fool around in class and to get their assignments done.

As one can see by my sample lesson plan calendar, it is full on a daily basis. What students don't get done in class is sometimes scheduled for homework. Sometimes students are excused from doing an assignment because time did not allow it to be covered in class. The point is, teachers should always have more assignments scheduled than students can complete in a class period.

Some lessons may take longer or less time than the teacher's plan. For shorter assignments that do not take the entire period as planned, teachers can rely on pending work from the lessons that were not completed from previous class periods.

Part of keeping students on task is having a daily calendar of activities in which students have a copy and/or access to on-line. Students should always know what is going to take place before entering any class.

As explained in this book, part of my daily routine is to have my assistant supervisor read the daily assignment calendar for the activities that will take place that day as a reminder. Also my assistant supervisor will read the activities that will take place during the next class period along with the assignments that are due at that time.

When students are on task and well-informed, they tend to behave better in class. Believe it or not, I still have students say, "I was absent last class. What did I miss?" or "I will be out next class period. What will I miss?"

My response is "Check your assignment calendar" or "Let's check your assignment calendar together."

All in all, students are generally well-informed about the daily assignments. They express appreciation to me for being so prepared with activities and for providing each student with a copy of the activity calendar.

Along with having well-prepared students, making class leaders out of students with conduct issues can also help with classroom management. At the beginning of each year or rotation of students, teachers can closely observe students and seek out the loud or disruptive students. They can then encourage these students to apply for leadership roles or appoint them as one of the class leaders. Miraculously, students change their behavior when given a leadership role along with receiving praise for their good behavior and performance in that role.

In addition to making class leaders out of students with conduct issues, having a system where students can get *"perfect day"* points as a group can also help with classroom management. If no student has to sign the disciplinary log during a class period, the entire class will get bonus points for that specific day. This process (explained further in this book) encourages students to help his or her peers behave properly. Some classes strive more than others to obtain perfect day points, but the point is, the class as a whole is striving toward a common goal of a perfect day.

There are many techniques to limit behavior issues in a classroom, and many are done by trial and error. Teachers should try many techniques until finding a technique that works best for each class period. Each class has its own personality.

Within this book, many techniques are explained that can keep classrooms running smoothly. I don't suggest trying to implement all of the procedures at once. Try two or three procedures at first, then work in an extra one each year.

Keep in mind that these classroom procedures have been developed over a period of many years. Many of the forms were developed to keep my classroom well-managed, on task, and to assist me in helping students stay organized. Having a system in place allows me the ability to issue important papers that come from the administrative office, make important announcements, and remind students when they have missing assignments.

An organized teacher who trains students to become organized will in turn have an organized and well-managed classroom with well-behaved students.

Chapter Four

Technology and Collaboration

Technology is changing the education process and how instruction is delivered inside and outside the classroom. With the emergence of online books, many districts are moving away from printed textbooks and using eBooks.

Many teachers who taught courses without district-issued textbooks had used a variety of resources and other aids in teaching students. This method of teaching is changing rapidly. For many years, colleges have adapted a platform of online courses, and this process has made its way into the secondary education arena. More and more secondary online schools are emerging.

Many platforms can be used for online instruction, almost too many to count. Today, school districts and employers, especially career and technology education programs, want students to be ready for the workforce. Employers today want students to enter the workforce with academic knowledge and training in how to collaborate, communicate, critically think, and be creative, known as the 4C's.

Houston ISD sponsored a Transformation Institute - Summer 2015. Teachers learned many valuable technology tools that will help students master the four Cs. Below is a list of free online resources that were provided, which can be used in each of the above areas.

It is beyond the scope of this book to discuss the uses of all these tools. Teachers can attend many workshops that will address the tools, and information is available online.

Although the list below has a number of free resources, there are many others that teachers can investigate for a cost.

Collaboration:	**Communication:**		**Creativity:**
Office 365	Animoto	Storyjumper	Popplet
Google Docs	Linoit	Voicethread	Prezi
Wikispaces	Popplet	**Critical Thinking:**	Animoto
Twiducate	Prezi	Popplet	Linoit
Bubble.us	Skype	Prezi	Blabberize
Screencastomatic	Voki	Edupuzzle	Answergarden
Stormboard	Twiducate	Blabberize	Bigmaker
Poetica	Edublogs	Powtoons	Powtoons
Tackk	Bigmarker	Padlet	Storyjumper
	Nearpod	Quizlet	Weebly
	Screencastomatic	Socrative	
	Eyejot	Weebly	

I use a variety of technology-based tools in my classroom. Each day (every other cycle) my students present health-related current event articles. Students used to post their article for all of their classmates to read via Edmodo®, and their peers can respond and collaborate about the article. Edmodo is currently a platform where students and teachers can post assignments and grades, and students and teachers can collaborate with each other.

I had my students turn in their article summary using Edmodo, so only I can read it and respond back with a grade for the assignment. Now my school district has a similar platform for my students to post and submit assignments. I also use Tunitin.com when students submit research reports and essays.

One of the presentations tools I have my students use is called Glogster®. Glogster allows students to do fantastic presentations displaying work, like a blog but in graphic format. Students have one page in which they can add hyperlinks, pictures, music, videos, etc. It was free when I first started using it, but now there is a cost. It is similar to Preszi®, which is free.

The technology tools I use for assessments are the E-instructions devices (for test), and Sentio® testing devices for quizzes. Students load their answer responses in the system, and when the assessment is complete, students can immediately see scores for their assessment. The grades can be exported into my electronic grade book. This saves me a tremendous amount of time over the traditional scantron grading and manually entering grades in my gradebook. Now my district has a similar platform that allows students to take test and quizzes on their own district-issued computers.

The HISD Transformation Institute provides teachers with great technology tools that help to manage multiple resources in one place.

Symbaloo® is a web tool that allows the user to bookmark multiple favorite websites in one location. Users can access their electronic bookmarks using Symbaloo from any computer, tablet, or smartphone with an internet connection. Teachers can bookmark sites for students to access.

Below are the links to three formulated Symbaloo pages with technology links for teachers. One beneficial feature in Symbaloo is the ability to research Symbaloo pages that have already been formulated with links for a particular subject.

Many of the technology tools listed above are found in the three Symbaloo links.

eTools for Education
http://www.symbaloo.com/mix/etoolsforeducation?searched=true

TOOLS for EDU
http://www.symbaloo.com/mix/tools-for-edu?searched=true

Tech for Teachers
http://www.symbaloo.com/mix/techforteachers?searched=true

Another useful, and free tool for students that I learned about at the HISD's Transformation Institute was a website called *vocabulary.com®*. Students could copy and paste an article in *vocabulary.com*, and it will display and define all of the vocabulary that is necessary to understand the article.

This tool is great for students reading at a lower level or reading difficult technical articles. The article review assignments incorporate the four Cs because students can "Collaborate" on each other's articles; students present (Communicate) the article they analyzed (using Critical thinking skills) to the class in a Creative manner.

One important secret to classroom management is keeping students engaged. An updated curriculum with lesson-plan content that utilizes current relevant topics, presented with the use of technology, will result in more students being actively engaged and fewer behavior violations.

Chapter Five

Become a Facilitator

Being a classroom facilitator allows students to take ownership of the class. Keep in mind that the end goal of the educational process is employment.

Start students off early by allowing them to work for you in the classroom facilitator. In any given class, students should be assigned jobs that will help the classroom run smoothly. With the exception of posting attendance, entering grades in the gradebook or computer, or lecturing on a very difficult academic content, students can do almost any job a teacher can do. When running a class like a business, it will flourish and grow into its own "fortune 500 company" for the school.

The process starts by assigning all students one job. Sometimes students may ask if they can have more than one job. This is not recommended unless the class is very small.

Within a particular class, more than one student can have the same job, such as the teacher assistant position. On form RMJ-18-Task/Duties Sign Up Sheet, teachers can record the names of the students filling the position on the line provided by each job description. These jobs were designed for a lab class but can be adapted for any class type.

The RMJ-18 form is only an example to give teachers ideas on how to create their own duties signup sheet. Students can also recommend jobs. Deciding how many students will be needed for each job will depend on the size of the class.

However for all classes, there should be only one supervisor, and two assistant supervisors. These can be elected positions by peer voting since most of the students know the abilities and accomplishments of their peers. Students can volunteer for the majority of the positions. Teachers can also appoint students to these positions, especially the students who are identified as problematic or outspoken.

Important positions have a way of turning around a student with a behavior problem. Before beginning the process, explain to students the duties of each job and how many students are needed for each job. There is a PowerPoint of the duties and responsibilities provided with the electronic material on the publisher's' website to aid in explaining each job.

When it comes to the volunteer positions and you have five students volunteering for the same job that requires only two. The "Rock-Paper-Scissors" game normally works well.

After all the positions have been assigned, train the students to do their jobs. It normally takes a few weeks for students to get the hang of doing their job correctly and efficiently before the class can run smoothly.

At this time, videos of the students doing their jobs are only shown at the classroom management seminar/workshops. Soon videos will be available at the publisher's website.

In addition to assigning all students jobs, teachers should also assign students to teach a lesson or activity. In a lab class, assign students to demonstrate the lab along with a PowerPoint or some other visual presentation format for the lab.

I started this process one day when I had several different serology tests to demonstrate, so I had each table demonstrate a test kit. I was astonished to see that the students were very attentive when their peers were presenting. The students were more attentive than when I demonstrated.

I decided to adopt this method for all of my labs and have a process where each student is a "teacher for a day." At the beginning of each rotation, I assign students a lab to demonstrate. For the most part, the students' seat numbers are the labs they will demonstrate. I have eleven labs. The students in seats 12 and above will co-teach with the students in seats 1-11.

I normally have a quiz at the beginning of each period for my lab class, and the teacher of the day must start their quiz as soon as they enter the class. While their peers are taking their quiz, I teach students how to demonstrate the lab to the class.

Sometimes students come in during their lunch period or after school to practice their lab in order to be a great teacher for their peers. After the demonstration is over, the "teachers of the day" are my student helpers and assist their peers in completing their lab.

Instead of students calling on me for help, they ask their peer teachers. It is great to see students taking that leadership role. Some years I give a "Teacher of the Year" or "Teacher of the Rotation" award.

For the microbiology unit, students do a presentation on how they identified their unknown organisms. The presentation includes explaining the various types of media, the flow chart of how they identified their unknown, along with the principle and procedure of all the tests done to identify their unknown organism.

Students normally do much better on their microbiology test because they have become teachers of the subject. This process works well for me.

Having a system in place for students to do peer teaching and assigning jobs to all students are two great ways to become a class facilitator. As teachers develop this process, it will make the educational experience more valuable and rewarding for both the students and the teachers.

Chapter Six:
How to Get Students Off to a Great Start the First Four Days of School

This chapter is the outline of the step-by-step process that is used when conducting a classroom management seminar/workshop. The information in parentheses are the RMJ forms that are included in the book. Some of the *RMJ forms are available on the publisher's website and are electronically formatted and customizable.

I. **1st Day of School**

   A. As students enter the room, direct students to their pre-assigned seat number.
      Use *RMJ-1 to put numbers on the students' desks. Inform students that seat numbers are temporary and will change with schedules or behavior issues.
   B. Get acquainted with your students.
      1. Do a get-acquainted game with your students. (My favorite is the adjective/name game.)
      2. Give winner(s) of the games a bonus hall pass (RMJ-2).
      3. Also give a bonus hall pass to students who had parents attend open house. (Give students the open house date ASAP.)
   C. Do any necessary school business (enrollment forms, lunch applications, etc.).
   D. Review Course Overview/Syllabus (See RMJ-Sample-1).
      1. Discuss required supplies.
      2. Use RMJ-3 to record the required supplies (if applicable).

II. **2nd Day of School**

   A. Review Grading Policy. (See RMJ-Sample-2). When students know what is expected by the teacher, most students will live up to the teacher's expectations.
      1. Review how students' grades will be determined and any issues that will affect students' grades.
         a. Explain the process for late work and how late work will affect the student's grades.
         b. Explain the Excuse Forms (RMJ-4) or (RM-35J Late Log).
         c. Explain Student Late Work Filler (RMJ-5a or RMJ-5b). Make copies in class colors.
         d. Use Missing or Absent Filler (RMJ-6) when student fails to turn in RMJ-5 or when a student is absent. Make copies in red.
         e. Information about the students mailbox slots are available at www.JacksonService.Biz
      2. Review tardy policy.

a. Review consequences for tardies.
   b. Review Tardy Log (*RMJ-7) and how students should sign it.
   c. Use Detention Assignment Form (RMJ-8) if you have to assign students detention for tardies or conduct restoration.
3. Review Conduct policy.
   a. Review consequences for conduct violations.
   b. Reviews Conduct Log (*RMJ-9) and how students should sign it.
4. Review Professionalism Policy (if applicable).
   a. Review consequences for professionalism violations
   b. Review Professionalism Log (*RMJ-10) or RMJ-10a and how students should sign it.
   c. Review Paychecks (RMJ-10b) (if applicable).
5. Use Temporary Log Sheet (RMJ-11) for tardies, conduct, and professionalism violations until class schedules are stable. Use RMJ-34 (formerly RMJ 11a) as a cover for your log books.
6. Review Extra Credit Policy (if applicable).
   a. Discuss what students can do to earn extra credit.
   b. Use Extra Credit Log (*RMJ-12) to keep tract.

B. Review the policy for being excused from class.
   1. Discuss Sign Out Sheet (RMJ-13).
   2. Explain to students how to use their personal hall pass (RMJ-14).
   3. Give bonus points to students who do not use their personal hall pass. Just write seat numbers on hall passes until students need to use it so that you can recycle passes and only replace the passes that are used.
   4. Sign-In Sheet (RMJ-15) can be posted in your class and used for students who constantly interrupt your class by visiting with other students.

C. Give out Parent Signature Forms (*RMJ-16)
   a. Require students to return the next class period.
   b. If students forget, give students one additional day to return form or sign the conduct log each class day until form is returned. Students can end up with a documented "P" in conduct for not returning a required parent signature document.
   c. Encourage students to have their parents register their email address with you. This is an excellent way to reach parents.
   d. Give Bonus Hall Pass (RMJ-2) as an incentive.

III. **3rd Day of School**

A. Have students complete Personal Data Sheets (RMJ-17) if students' schedules and information are not assessable in a database.
   1. Explain to the students that personal data sheets will be used for letters of recommendations, rotation slots, job inquiries etc. This may encourage students to behave professionally in class.
   2. Discuss evaluation and Letter of Recommendation (*RMJ-Sample-3).

3. All students should have classroom responsibilities. (Conduct your class like a business, especially if it is a job-training class). Be a facilitator more than a teacher.
   a. Review duties with students.
   b. Assign classroom duties and record on Duties Sign-Up Sheet (RMJ-18).
   c. Use Daily Duties Log Sheet (RMJ-19) to give students a grade or bonus points for doing and recording their daily duties.

B. Discuss daily routine (If time permits. If not, discuss on day four.)
   - After the tardy bell rings, the teacher will welcome students and announce that students have two minutes to turn in homework assignments (if any) to their mailbox slot. After two minute, the teacher or mailbox technician will pick up all work from mail slots. All slots should have student work or filler sheet form unless a student is absent. If a student is absent, the teacher or mailbox technician will put the Missing/Absent Filler (RMJ-6) in the mail slot before retrieving work from the mail slots. Have students put their Excuse Forms (RMJ-4) in the color-coded class folder, which should be located on or near teacher's desk. Use the Excuse Forms (RMJ-4) for parent conferences, and the form can be used at open house and at a mass conference. (Process shown at workshops only.)
   - After assignments (if any) are collected, the supervisor will come forward and read the supervisor script (*RMJ-20) on the front of the attendance log book. The class can be set up where the supervisor automatically comes forward or the teacher calls the supervisor forward. The supervisor takes attendance using the student attendance log book (only names, no ID numbers) and gives attendance to teacher for verification. The teacher will verify attendance and post attendance in computer or record it in teacher's official grade book. Also, part of the supervisor script includes having all students check their area for trash and report trash on Daily Clean Up Log (RMJ-23).
   - Assistant supervisor #1 is called forward to read the supervisor script 1 (*RMJ-21), which should be posted on the wall by the assignment calendar. This will include reading the assignment calendar for the current day and next class period. Sometimes one week in advance will be read if a major assignment is due. All students will write or highlight the assignment and due date on Daily Assignment Sheet (*RMJ-22) as it is being read. (Make sure students understand that the assignment sheet is part of students' notebook grade.)
   - Assistant supervisor #2 will be called forward to read script 2 (*RMJ-21), also on a wall next to the students' handout baskets. Supervisor #2 will also be responsible for reading any announcements and delegating (via the teacher's instructions) the passing out of papers that the teacher placed in students' baskets for that class. Supervisor #2 will also call students forward by calling out seat numbers from the Student Summons Page (RMJ-28).
   - The first fifteen to twenty minutes of class time should be an ongoing assignment (student questions, warm up, etc.). Students should always know what to do, and students get focused at the beginning of class. This gives the teacher time to get situated, post attendance, etc.

IV. **4th Day of School**

    A. Discuss student notebook.
        1. Make a cover page for each class notebook. A different color should be used for each class and recycled each year until a new copy is needed. Include on the cover page the name of the school, address, title of course, and room number. If the students' notebook gets lost or left on the bus, it can be returned to the student. (See sample notebook at the end of the seminar.)
        2. Provide students with a title page for their notebook (*RMJ 32; formerly RMJ-24a). As soon as the notebook is open, it will reveal the student who owns the notebook.
        3. Make a notebook Table of Contents for all papers you issue to students, and have students put their notebook together using the notebook Table of Contents. (See sample 4.)
        4. Discuss grade sheets (*RMJ-24)
        5. Discuss notebook grade sheets (*RMJ-25)

V. Lesson Plans
    1. Use form *RMJ-26 to make a lesson plan calendar so students can have a printed copy of the lesson plan calendar. Use the same lesson plan calendar each year; just change the dates from year to year. Students can highlight the assignments as the assistant supervisor is reading the assignment each day. (See RMJ-26-Sample.)
    2. Use form *RMJ-27 to make lesson plans. Make one lesson plan for each day. Some plans can expand over a two-day period. The lesson plan can be used and modified each year. Use the same lesson plan calendar each year. (See RMJ-5-Sample.)

All forms are copyrighted material. Please do not share copies. Only workshop attendees and purchasers of book are allowed to make copies of items to use in their classrooms.

Rosters of all workshop attendees are kept on file. Please direct interested teachers to www.JacksonServices.Biz to obtain a copy of the classroom management book and electronic documents.

I hope you can use some of the classroom management strategies. It may take a few years to slowly add most of the strategies to your class routine. These strategies work well for me, but everyone must find what works best for their classroom set up.

I have very few failures and very few parent conference. I also have many more strategies, but time will not allow me to share them all. Please feel free to contact me via the company website at www.JacksonServices.Biz for more information concerning classroom management.

Thank you!

Chapter Seven
Rational Behind the Various Logs and Sheets Developed

RMJ 1 - Numbers

Numbers 1-45 are provided. Heaven forbid if you ever have more than forty-five students in a class. The numbers serve several purposes. The numbers can be used on the following:
- Student desks
- Student mail boxes
- Class sets of books and student book covers

Numbering student desks or tables allows teachers to direct students to an assigned seat on day one as they enter the classroom. Normally, class rosters are arranged in alphabetical order, which is the same order in which teachers enter grades in a computerized gradebook. It saves a tremendous amount of time when student seat numbers or classroom numbers are in alphabetical order. Some of my teachers refer to the numbers as classroom numbers not seat numbers. Students do not have to sit in alphabetical order, especially when teachers need to separate problem students.

Numbering the student mailbox stations allows students to turn in all work, parent signature documents, scantron, etc. to their mailbox slots so that items can be picked up in alphabetical order. Teachers can waste valuable time putting papers in alphabetical order to record grades in a gradebook or searching for the name in the gradebook to record a grade. Seconds add up to minutes, then hours, then days, etc.

Numbering class sets of books allows teachers to keep track of books assigned to students during class time. Numbering the covers on the books that the school checks out to the students allows teachers to quickly identify those books that students leave behind.

The numbers on the electronic version of RMJ-1 can have many other uses, and the numbers can be reduced or enlarged to meet the needs of the teacher.

RMJ 2 – Bonus Hall Pass

The bonus hall passes are useful only when students have a limited number of passes to leave the classroom. Bonus hall passes are given so that a student can have emergency passes instead of their regular hall passes. The regular hall passes can be cashed in for an incentive at the end of the semester or rotation. Bonus hall passes are given to students at the beginning of the school year or rotation as a prize for the get-acquainted games. If a parent attends open house and/or if their parents register their email address, then the student can earn bonus hall passes.

RMJ 3– Supply Track

At the beginning of each school year, students are given their list of required supplies for the course (i.e., tissue boxes for freshman classes and for medical lab classes, disinfecting wipes, paper towels, alcohol and alcohol swabs, etc). The form was developed because after the first or second week of the course, students forgot about bringing the required supplies. The semester came to an end and supplies from only the few students were collected.

> *I started posting the "Thanks for bringing required supplies" sheet as a reminder to ask students about their required supplies in addition to a quick way of tracking which students brought in their required supplies. I print out a roster the day I begin collecting supplies, and students with supplies sign their names next to their seat numbers for that day. In the days that follow, students may have a different seat number, however; students sign their names next to the seat numbers according to the printed roster as supplies arrive daily. At a glance, I can see which students brought the required supplies and which students were pending with their supplies.*

RMJ 4– Excuse form or *RMJ-35 Late Log (*Developed the 2014/15 school year)

This excuse form or *late log was designed as a way of keeping track of students who were late or failed to turn in an assignment. It serves as the teacher's documentation that the student did or did not turn in an assignment.

> *The worst feeling I had as a teacher, was a student saying to me, "Mrs. Jackson, I turned in my assignment. You must have missed placed it."*
>
> *Did I, or did the students not turn in the assignment? Well, the excuse form or late log is proof that the students did or did not turn in the assignment as least on the day it was due.*

The excuse form or late log is used in the event of a parent conference so that the parent can see the documentation of their child's reason(s) for not turning in his/her assignments as well as the number of times assignments were turned in late.

The teacher and/or school must have a policy in place that establishes the number of days a student can be delinquent turning in a late assignments. When students are allowed to turn in late assignments at any time, it can be very stressful on a teacher, especially when many students are turning in various missing assignments the last week of the cycle once they realize they have a less-than-desirable or failing grade.

The school in which I am employed has a policy that after two school days, late assignments are no longer accepted. It forces students to stay on track, and teachers can keep a handle on grades. If a school is on block scheduling, and the students meet every other day, and an assignment is due on Monday and is not turned in, the student has until Wednesday to turn in the assignment, or it becomes a zero. It is very important that a firm deadline is given to the students and parents establishing when late work is no longer accepted. An exception has to be allowed when students are out for an extended period of time.

Stories are always circulating about teachers who do not adhere to a policy on late work. At the end of the grading cycle, that teacher is swamped with grading late assignments in addition to any end-of-the-cycle or semester assessments. Late work is one of the most challenging issues that teachers face. Teachers who adhere to their late policy are on easy street at the end of the cycle. Teachers should not lead students to believe that life beyond high school won't have consequences when students are late on assignments in college, on the job, and with paying bills, etc. As adults, we know that is not the case. Students should also know that they will be held accountable for being late on an assignment, to class, school, etc.

RMJ 5– Late work filler and late work log

The late work filler was designed to be a filler in the place of a missing assignment. It is a placeholder and reminder that assignments are still outstanding.

The filler pages stand out in a stack of papers if the filler pages are color coded. Anytime a student does not have an assignment, students will put in a filler page in their mailbox slots in the place of their work. My filler pages are normally color coded to my class color, and I give students a few sheets to keep in their notebook. At a glance, I can tell if I have late or missing assignments and in what class because the colored late work filler pages stand out.

The next class period, which is the final day that assignments will be accepted, I call for the missing assignments and either exchange the late work filler for the late assignments and check "yes" for receiving the late assignment or check "no" if the assignment is not turned in.

When assignments are returned, the students receives their filler page back with a "no" checked. Students know to record a grade of zero in their grade sheet for that assignment.

RMJ 6– Missing/Absent Fillers (Make copies in Red to stand out)

The missing or absent fillers serve the same purpose as the late work filler except that the students are absent and cannot compete the form. Therefore, it must be completed by the teacher or the mailbox technician.

Occasionally, classroom teachers will have to complete the form when students escape the classroom without turning in an assignment at the end of the period. This situation normally happens when assignments are due at the end of class.

For this reason, it is best to have assignments turned in at least five minutes before the dismissal bell. All assignments can be accounted for along with any late work fillers that the students will complete or absent fillers that can be completed by the teacher or mailbox technician.

As the technology age advances, students will be turning in assignments electronically, and forms, such as the late work and missing/absent fillers, will become obsolete. Until then, these forms can be useful tools to keep track of those assignments not submitted on time or not at all.

RMJ 7– Tardy Log

The purpose of the tardy log is to keep track of students who are tardy to class. It is designed for the student and teacher to keep tract of tardies and see the consequences for each tardy. It is important that students understand the importance of being on time to class. Teachers should hold students accountable for their actions just as the real world will hold them accountable as employees.

The tardy policy should be explained to the students at the beginning of the course and be part of the grading policy. Parents and students should sign the policy. It is the responsibility of the classroom teacher to enforce the tardy policy. Students quickly learn which classes they can be tardy to and which ones they must be on time.

RMJ 8– Detention Log

The detention log was designed as a way to track assigned detention days for students who were assigned detention due to excessive tardies. Now it is used for conduct restoration.

RMJ 9– Conduct Log

The conduct log was designed for documenting each offense with the student's initials along with the date and the conduct code violated. Just like the tardy log, the teacher and students can see the consequence as each conduct violation is documented. Parent notices are normally sent out via email or via the professionalism paycheck (RMJ 10b) to parents without an email address.

RMJ 10– Professionalism Log

The Professionalism log was designed to keep track of student violations of the ten professionalism rules of our health science department. Each offense is documented, and the students initial the log along with the date and the professionalism code violated. Just like the tardy log, the teacher and students can see the consequence as each professionalism violation is documented.

Parent notices are normally sent out via email or via the professionalism pay check (RMJ 10b) to parents without an email address. Because health science is considered a career and technology course, teachers are allowed to give professionalism grades, which in the health science department is ten percent of the students' overall grades.

At the beginning of the school year, the importance of being professional on a job (in our case, a job training course) is stressed. Professionalism rules are part of the grading policy signed by students and parents.

> *Here is a little side story to share a past experience with you. When I first started teaching, I was told that ten percent of the students' grades was based on professionalism. I began my teaching career the last nine weeks of the school year without any training on teaching techniques, classroom management, or school policy. When students misbehaved, I took points off their professionalism grade because coming from the healthcare industry, our professional evaluations were based on our conduct and performance on the job.*
>
> *A student challenged me one day and told me that I could not take points off of his grade for misbehavior. My first year, students challenged me for everything. It got so bad that one day a student ran out of my class without permission and ran to the principal*

and told her, "... students can't learn anything in her class because she's always in conflict with students..."

My principal called me to her office immediately and asked me if this was the case. I told her, "Yes," and exclaimed that "the students will not listen to me."

My principal also explained that she was told I was taking points off students' weekly professional grade for conduct issues.

I explained, "That is correct. I was told that ten percent of students' grades was professionalism, and I'm doing what I was told to do."

Much to my disappointment, the principal then explained to me that my students were indeed correct. I could not take points off of their grade for conduct issues, and conduct issues should be reflected in the students' conduct grades.

Wow, was I shocked or what? My principal and I created ten golden professionalism rules that I used in my classroom, which happened to be a lab class at the time. To this day, I still use the rules, and they have been adopted into the grading policy for our health-science department.

When the grading policy is discussed with students and parents at the beginning of the school year, the difference between the professionalism rules and conduct rules is explained. It is also emphasized that in the real world, job performance and evaluations are both based on conduct and professionalism. The statement from the grading policy read as follows:

> In Health Science, you will be receiving a six-week cycle Professionalism Grade that will count as ten percent of your total grade. Students are expected to conduct themselves in a professional and courteous manner at all times. In real-life job situations, employees are evaluated on performance and professionalism. Excellent evaluations on a job usually will result in awards and promotions in pay, rank, or both. Poor evaluations may result in either a demotion in pay or rank or being fired.
>
> The rules below must be followed in order to prevent losing points from your Professionalism Grade. You will begin each six weeks with 100 points. Ten (10) points will be taken off each time you violate one of the professionalism rules. Students are allowed to write positive sentences to restore professionalism grades with three days of violation. See Teacher. Every week, students will receive a Professionalism Grade Paycheck.

RMJ 10b– Professionalism paycheck

The professionalism paycheck was designed to give students their professionalism grade in a fun and realistic manner. Many people get paid on Friday, so professionalism paychecks are issued on Fridays as well. Students really get a kick out of getting a paycheck each week.

Students are told that parent signatures are optional. However, students are rewarded with bonus points if they return the check the very next class period with a parent signature. Bonus points are not given after the second day. Students are required to return their paychecks that have boxes checked stating the following:

- **One more conduct violation = "S" in conduct**
- **One more conduct violation = "P" in conduct**
- **Student failing or at risk: Current average _____**

RMJ 11– Temporary Log Sheet

The Temporary Log Sheet was designed to be used the first three weeks of school when the courses are not yet set in stone. After students' schedules are final, students sign their names next to their seat numbers on all of the log sheets. Information is transferred from the temporary log RMJ-11 to the permanent log sheets. Not many students sign form RMJ-11 because they are given a grace period for the first two or three weeks of school to get accustomed to the rules.

When students break a rule during the grace period, they are reminded that this is grace week, and the consequences are discussed as well as what will happen when the grace period is over. Students do know that during grace week they cannot earn any "perfect day" points.

> *In some of my junior twelve-week rotations, I ask students after two weeks of a grace period if they want to continue one more week of a grace period or start earning perfect day points.*

Perfect Day Points

Students are told that in the real world when company employees are on task and work together to get the job done, productivity is usually high. These companies sometimes reward employees with end-of-the-year bonuses. However when productivity is low, it is not always due to the economy. It may be due to the employees' low productivity, and in most cases result in employees being fired for poor performance of the job. Layoffs normally follow because the company's profits decline.

Students can receive one bonus point each day **_all_** students are on task for the day. That means that no student was tardy, no assignments were missing, and no rules were broken, etc.

> *My students and I discuss situations in which they can look out for each other.*
> *I ask, "If you see your classmate chewing gum in the lab, what do you do?"*
> *Most students get the point and respond, "Tell the classmate to spit out his her gum before Ms. Jackson sees him or her."*
> *We also discuss situations that when one or more classmates are always late or missing assignments, what should students do? We discuss solutions such as offer assistance, tell them their study and homework routine (not do the work for them), or form study groups etc.*
> *At the end of the discussion, I ask, "Are you your brother's keeper?"*
> *Most students respond, "Yes."*
> *The purpose for my perfect-day system is to get my class working together like a great company would work together. Remember, I run my class like a business. The catch to the perfect-day point is someone in the class must ask me at the end of the period if the class received perfect-day points. I would immediately write the bonus in pencil in the extra credit log. I tell students if any trash is found, I will be erasing the bonus point.*

RMJ 12– Extra Credit Log

The Extra Credit Log was designed keep track of all the bonus points students earned.

RMJ 13– Student Sign Out Log

The Sign-Out Log was designed for students who leave during class for appropriate personal needs. If a parent, administrator, counselor, etc. comes in or calls for a student, then teachers can look at the sign-out log and state the location of the student.

In large and busy classes, teachers may not always remember where students are going. The log can be documentation in the event a particular student's behavior becomes questionable. If a student is always leaving the class, especially around the same time every day, it creates a pattern on the part of the student.

It states at the bottom of the Sign-Out Sheet that copies may be sent to the office, counselor, and/ or nurse to be explored for medical or substance abuse problems. The statement at the bottom of the log makes students aware of the fact that student behaviors are being monitored.

RMJ 14 – Hall Pass

The hall passes are designed for students to use six times during the semester or rotation.

> *The reason I designed the hall passes is because I used to have one student behind the other leave my class for one reason or another.*
> *I always asked, "Is it an emergency?"*
> *Of course the answer was always, "Yes."*
> *With the hall passes, students decide if their leaving the class is an emergency. The pressure was taken from me and put on the student.*
> *My goal was to have all of my students in class learning and not leaving the class unless it was an emergency. Since I developed the hall passes, most of my student stay in class and never use their hall pass. However, I do give an incentive for students to not use their hall pass, and I recycle the unused passes.*
> *Since my students are grade-driven, I give bonus points.*

Teachers have to get to know their students and find out what would motivate them to only use their hall pass for an emergency.

RMJ 15– Student Sign In Log

This log was designed to keep students from interrupting my class to visit with another student.

> *Students interrupting my class used to be a problem for me when I first started teaching. The last form I put on my wall faded because not many students were interrupting my class to visit with another student. Students had to sign the time they arrived to my class and from which class they were coming. I no longer need to use the form.*

This is a great log to put on you wall for a while. The problem with students interrupting classes to visit with other students will eventually go away.

RMJ 16 a and b – Parent Signature Documents (Teacher Copy and Parent Copy)

This document was designed to have documentation that the students and parents are aware of the grading policy and the consequences. It is very important to make sure to collect ***all students/parent signature documents.*** It becomes valuable at parent/teachers conferences.

RMJ 17– Information and Student Evaluation Sheet

This sheet was designed to give students feedback on their performance outside of the normal conduct and academic grade. It should be kept on file for a few years and can be used for student letters of recommendation. It can be used when an employer calls and wants to know how a student performed in a career preparation course.

> *Once I had a former student come back and tell me they had to have an evaluation from their health-science lab teacher. I shared this with my students and told them that I may be called upon to answer questions on their behalf, even if I wasn't listed as a reference or asked to write a letter of recommendation.*

This form encourages students to be on their best behavior because students never know when a teacher may have to give an evaluation that the student didn't request.

RMJ 18– Class Duties Sign Up Sheet

This form was designed for teachers to keep track of students' job assignments so that by assigning ***all*** students a job, they can run their class like a business. Students write their official job titles and their job descriptions on the title pages of their notebooks RMJ-32.

Some students have a daily routine for their job such as the supervisor, assistant supervisor, and a few others. All other students are called forward when their job needs to be performed.

If students can't remember their jobs when called upon by the teacher, they can simply look on the title page of their notebooks to determine if they are being summoned to complete their tasks for the day.

The sheet should be kept handy in case students do not come forward when their job title is called.

RMJ 19– Daily Duties Log Sheet

This form was designed to have students check off on their daily duties. Again in the real world, some employees have a duties-task sheet, maintenance log, or something to check off daily. This is part of job training.

Teachers can use the completed form as a daily grade or award bonus points for students who check off a determined number (i.e., ten checks of daily duties) during a semester or rotation.

*RMJ 20– Directions for Supervisor

The supervisor script was designed so that the class supervisor knows what to say each day to guide the class at the beginning of each class period.

*RMJ 21– Directions for Assistant Supervisor

The assistant supervisor script was designed so that the assistant supervisors know what to say each day to guide the class at the beginning of each class period.

RMJ 22– Cycle Assignment Calendar

This form was designed for students to write down and keep track of their daily assignments.

RMJ 23– Daily Clean Up Log

This log was designed to keep track of students leaving trash behind. It is a professionalism violation for students who fail to clean up their immediate surrounding before leaving class.

RMJ 24– Grade Sheet

This form was designed for students to keep track of their grades.

> *Before my school district had the online gradebook, the only way students could keep track of their grades was to write it down and calculate it manually. At the end of the cycle, I had students calculate their grade by hand. I checked the students' calculated grades with my manual or spreadsheet computer grades to see if both grades matched. I was able to catch any grading errors on my part.*
>
> *Now, due to the online gradebook, students and parents can see grades online, but I still have students write down all returned grades on their grade sheet so that they can verify if their grades were recorded correctly.*
>
> *As a teacher, I do make mistakes, and I tell students it is now their responsibly to verify all grades online and report any discrepancies to me ASAP.*

RMJ 25– Notebook Grade Sheet Sample

This sheet was designed so that students know what to expect for their notebook check. The notebook check is a major grade. The notebook grade sheet states how many points each item in the notebook is worth. Students first do a self-check worth five points before the final check.

RMJ 26– Cycle Lesson Plan Calendar

This cycle lesson plan calendar was created so that students can see all assignments for the cycle.

> *I first started using the RMJ-22, or the blank assignment calendar. Students would write their assignments from my lesson plan calendar; however, too many students did not write their assignments down and were not prepared for class.*
>
> *I started populating a regular month calendar with student assignments and giving a copy to my students. I had ten pages of lesson plan calendars from August through May. At one PLC meeting, I got the idea from Mr. Desai, a math teacher at my school, to do a cycle lesson plan calendar. So instead of using ten pages of a regular calendar, I had six cycle calendars.*

With this calendar format, students can see all their assignments, test, and quizzes for an entire cycle.

RMJ 27– Lesson Plan Form

The lesson plans (LP) were originally designed for one day-one lesson with all of the objectives, activities, materials, assessments, etc. needed to compete the lesson for the day. Pages were titled Day 1 Lesson Plan, Day 2 Lesson Plan, etc.

Day 1 LP was the first day of school, Day 2 LP, the second day of school, etc. Design changes were made to retitle the lesson plans to state "Lesson Plan 1," "Lesson Plan 2," etc., with each covering a certain set of objectives.

A LP page can cover two or three class days. For example, Lesson Plan 5 may take Monday and Wednesday to complete. It is also designed so that lesson plan pages do not necessary have to go in calendar order.

The Assignment Plan Calendar (RMJ-26) corresponds to the detailed Lesson Plan Form. Dates are not written on the Lesson Plan Form, only Lesson Plan 1, 2 etc. With this design, once a lesson page is created with the objectives that need to be covered, the lesson plan only has to be created once.

Teachers can use the Lesson Plan Forms over and over and only make minor adjustments each year if any. The more generic teachers title the assignments, the fewer adjustments to the Lesson Plan Form need to be made.

For example, teachers can have an Activity 1 or a Quiz 1 for each unit. Teachers can change Activity 1 as many times as needed to keep the course fresh and undated without changing the Lesson Plan Form.

The Lesson Plan Form will save teachers volumes of time when it comes to creating lesson plans. Make sure to see the example lesson plan form and sample cycle assignment calendar. Remember the more generic, the better.

> *I started adding more and more information and titling assignments over the years making my Lesson Plan Form less generic, but I am reverting back to a more generic plan. Less is more efficient when it comes to lesson planning.*

One of the most important considerations in effective lesson planning is stating the objectives of the lesson and having assignments and assessments for the objectives.

RMJ-28 Student Summons Page (RMJ-28 was formally the survey sheet)

This page is designed for the assistant supervisor to call students forward to see the teacher for reasons listed on the sheet. The assistant supervisor will call students forward by their seat number and then hand the form to the teacher as a reminder as to why students were called forward.

RMJ-29 Broken Item Log

This log was designed to keep track of items that the school provided that were broken due to student negligence, especially in lab classes.

RMJ-30 Typo Log

This log was designed to have students help teachers find typos in lecture notes. Bonus points can be awarded to the first students to find a typo. This system encourages students to read the lecture notes carefully.

RMJ-31 Student Permit

This form was designed to have a standard permit for a school, department, or individual teacher to use. It is designed for students who want to go to another teacher's class during a homeroom period, tutorial period, etc. Both teachers sign or initial the permit. It can also be used to send students to the library during class, send students to lunch, or for any reason that might be needed.

RMJ 32–Notebook Title Page (Formally RMJ-24a)

This sheet was designed so that the owner of a lost student notebook can be identified based on the first page in the notebook along with the class, the seat number assigned to the student, the job title assigned to the student, etc.

RMJ 33– Key for Notebook/Student Portfolio Tabs

This sheet was designed as a title page for tabs to help students keep an organized and neat notebook.

*RMJ-34-Log Book Cover sheet (Formally RMJ-11a)

The log book cover was designed for use with a binder that has a sheet protective cover in the front and on the sides.

*RMJ-35 Late Log

This late log was designed as a way of keeping track of students who are late or fail to turn in an assignment.

*RMJ-36 Standardized Testing Management Process

This information sheet was designed to aid teachers who proctor standardized test.

Available in electronic format on the publisher's website for free or for a small fee are:

Customizable RMJ forms
Sample Letter of Recommendation and criteria sheet
Welcome Sign for classroom door and Sample Room Signs
Sample Notebook Table of Contents
Sample Lesson Plans
Sample Lesson Plan Calendar
Sample Course Overview/Syllabus
Sample Welcome PPT for 1st Day of School
Sample Welcome PPT for Open House
Other Miscellaneous forms and word documents I used for classroom management

References

Charles, C. M. (2005). Barbara Coloroso's Inner Discipline. *Classroom Discipline* (8th ed., p. 147). Boston: Person Education.

Charles, C. M. (2005). Linda Albert's Cooperative Discipline. *Classroom Discipline* (8th ed., p. 200-201). Boston: Person Education.

Classroom Management. (n.d.). Retrieved September 23, 2006, from Pacific Net Web site: http://www.pacificnet.net/~mandel/ClassroomManagement.html

Cooperative Learning. (n.d.). Retrieved June 29, 2006, from http://edtech.kennesaw.edu/intech/cooperativelearning.htm

Erlauer, L. (2003). *The Brain-Compatible Classroom* (p. 158). Alexandria, Virginia: Association for Supervision and Curriculum Development.

Gokhale, A. A. (2006, June). *Collaborative Learning Enhances Critical Thinking*. Retrieved June 29, 2006, from Digital Libraries and Archives Web site: http://scholar.lib.vt.edu/ejournals/JTE/jte-v7n1/gokhale.jte-v7n1.html

Seven Steps To Problem Solving. (n.d.). Retrieved June 29, 2006, from http://www.pitt.edu/~groups/probsolv.html

Shlomo, Sharan. (1990). *Cooperative Learning Theory and Research* (pp. 3-5). Westport, Connecticut: Praeger Publishers. Retrieved June 29, 2006, from http://www.questia.com/PM.qst?a=o&d=27218138 (SEVEN STEPS TO PROBLEM SOLVING)

Carla Theresa Mattioli. (1984, September). *Awakening Creative Behavior: Contributions from the Rudolf Steiner Method*. Retrieved September 9, 2006, from http://www.cct.umb.edu/abstracts.html

Churchward, B. (2003). *11 Techniques for Better Classroom Discipline*. Retrieved September 8, 2006, from Discipline By Design - The Level System Web site: http://www.honorlevel.com/techniques.xml

Facts About Corporal Punishment. (n.d.). Retrieved September 9, 2006, from National Coalition to Abolish Corporal Punishment in Schools (NCACPS) Web site: http://www.stophitting.com/disatschool/facts.php

Teacher Talk, Volume 1, Issue 2 :What is your classroom management profile? (Last Updated: December 4, 2003). Retrieved October 7, 2006, from Indiana University - Center for Adolescent Studies, Web site: http://education.indiana.edu/cas/tt/v1i2/table.html

Pollan, Ryla, (n.d.). *Classroom Management Monopoly*. Retrieved October 7, 2006, from Pacific Net Web Web site: http://www.pacificnet.net/~mandel/ClassroomManagement.html

Freiberg, H. J. (1996). From Tourists to Citizens in the Classroom. *Educational Leadership, Volume 54* (Number 1), 32-36.

Mandel, Scott. (n.d.). *Classroom Set-Up: Grades 3-12*. Retrieved October 7, 2006, from Pacific Net Web Web site: http://www.pacificnet.net/~mandel/ClassroomManagement.html

1 2 3 4 5 6 7 8 9
10 11 12 13 14 15
16 17 18 19 20 21
22 23 24 25 26 27
28 29 30 31 32 33
34 35 36 37 38 39
40 41 42 43 44 45

Bonus Hall Passes RMJ-2

Please cut out and give to your students. Please make sure to put a colored seal/stamp to make it valid.

Bonus Hall Pass

This hall pass is awarded to:

____

Congratulations on earning your free pass. Please save this and use this in the place of your regular hall pass. To be valid, it must have a special colored stamp in the box above. Make sure you have the stamp upon receiving this award or inform your teacher immediately after receiving this pass, or it will not be valid.

Follow the normal procedure for being excused from class. Return this used bonus hall pass to your teacher after using it. ***Date used*** __________

Bonus Hall Pass

This hall pass is awarded to:

____

Congratulations on earning your free pass. Please save this and use this in the place of your regular hall pass. To be valid, it must have a special colored stamp in the box above. Make sure you have the stamp upon receiving this award or inform your teacher immediately after receiving this pass, or it will not be valid.

Follow the normal procedure for being excused from class. Return this used bonus hall pass to your teacher after using it. ***Date Used*** __________

Bonus Hall Pass

This hall pass is awarded to:

____

Congratulations on earning your free pass. Please save this and use this in the place of your regular hall pass. To be valid, it must have a special colored stamp in the box above. Make sure you have the stamp upon receiving this award or inform your teacher immediately after receiving this pass, or it will not be valid.

Follow the normal procedure for being excused from class. Return this used bonus hall pass to your teacher after using it. ***Date Used*** __________

Bonus Hall Pass

This hall pass is awarded to:

____

Congratulations on earning your free pass. Please save this and use this in the place of your regular hall pass. To be valid, it must have a special colored stamp in the box above. Make sure you have the stamp upon receiving this award or inform your teacher immediately after receiving this pass, or it will not be valid.

Follow the normal procedure for being excused from class. Return this used bonus hall pass to your teacher after using it. ***Date Used*** __________

Bonus Hall Pass

This hall pass is awarded to:

____

Congratulations on earning your free pass. Please save this and use this in the place of your regular hall pass. To be valid, it must have a special colored stamp in the box above. Make sure you have the stamp upon receiving this award or inform your teacher immediately after receiving this pass, or it will not be valid.

Follow the normal procedure for being excused from class. Return this used bonus hall pass to your teacher after using it. ***Date Used*** __________

Bonus Hall Pass

This hall pass is awarded to:

____

Congratulations on earning your free pass. Please save this and use this in the place of your regular hall pass. To be valid, it must have a special colored stamp in the box above. Make sure you have the stamp upon receiving this award or inform your teacher immediately after receiving this pass, or it will not be valid.

Follow the normal procedure for being excused from class. Return this used bonus hall pass to your teacher after using it. ***Date Used*** __________

Bonus Hall Pass

This hall pass is awarded to:

____

Congratulations on earning your free pass. Please save this and use this in the place of your regular hall pass. To be valid, it must have a special colored stamp in the box above. Make sure you have the stamp upon receiving this award or inform your teacher immediately after receiving this pass, or it will not be valid.

Follow the normal procedure for being excused from class. Return this used bonus hall pass to your teacher after using it. ***Date used*** __________

Bonus Hall Pass

This hall pass is awarded to:

____

Congratulations on earning your free pass. Please save this and use this in the place of your regular hall pass. To be valid, it must have a special colored stamp in the box above. Make sure you have the stamp upon receiving this award or inform your teacher immediately after receiving this pass, or it will not be valid.

Follow the normal procedure for being excused from class. Return this used bonus hall pass to your teacher after using it. ***Date Used*** __________

Thanks for bringing your required supplies!

Please sign your name next to the line that corresponds to your seat number on the attached roster.

1. _____
2. _____
3. _____
4. _____
5. _____
6. _____
7. _____
8. _____
9. _____
10. _____
11. _____
12. _____
13. _____
14. _____
15. _____
16. _____
17. _____
18. _____
19. _____
20. _____
21. _____
22. _____
23. _____
24. _____
25. _____
26. _____
27. _____
28. _____
29. _____
30. _____
31. _____
32. _____
33. _____
34. _____
35. _____
36. _____
37. _____
38. _____
39. _____
40. _____

RMJ-3

Excuse Forms: Please cut and make available by the students' mailbox stations.

Excuse Form for Failure to Submit Assignment

Name _____ Seat # _____
Teacher _____
Class _____
Period _____
Date _____

_____
Title of Assignment

The reason I do not have my assignment is as follows:
_____
_____

Excuse Blank Form for Failure to Submit Assignment

Name _____ Seat # _____
Teacher _____
Class _____
Period _____
Date _____

_____
Title of Assignment

The reason I do not have my assignment is as follows:
_____
_____

Excuse Blank Form for Failure to Submit Assignment

Name _____ Seat # _____
Teacher _____
Class _____
Period _____
Date _____

_____
Title of Assignment

The reason I do not have my assignment is as follows:
_____
_____

RMJ-4

Student Late Work Filler

Students not submitting the required work for today must:

- *Complete this **Late Work Filler Sheet** and complete an **Excuse Form**.*

- *Place filler sheet in student's mailbox slot within two minutes after teacher calls for assignment.*

- *Place the Excuse Form directly in your color-coded class folder, which is located on or near the teacher's desk.*

If this process is not complete within the required time, student will lose an additional 10 points off professionalism grade for not following instructions.

Any late work not submitted within the allotted time will result in a grade of zero (0). See grading policy.

When this filler sheet is returned to students, and the teacher has checked "No," the students should record a grade of zero (0) on grade sheet for that assignment.

			This section to be completed by teacher.
Seat #:____	Date:_____	Assignment:_____	Work Submitted: Yes ☐ No ☐ (Grade 0)
Seat #:____	Date:_____	Assignment:_____	Work Submitted: Yes ☐ No ☐ (Grade 0)
Seat #:____	Date:_____	Assignment:_____	Work Submitted: Yes ☐ No ☐ (Grade 0)
Seat #:____	Date:_____	Assignment:_____	Work Submitted: Yes ☐ No ☐ (Grade 0)
Seat #:____	Date:_____	Assignment:_____	Work Submitted: Yes ☐ No ☐ (Grade 0)
Seat #:____	Date:_____	Assignment:_____	Work Submitted: Yes ☐ No ☐ (Grade 0)
Seat #:____	Date:_____	Assignment:_____	Work Submitted: Yes ☐ No ☐ (Grade 0)
Seat #:____	Date:_____	Assignment:_____	Work Submitted: Yes ☐ No ☐ (Grade 0)
Seat #:____	Date:_____	Assignment:_____	Work Submitted: Yes ☐ No ☐ (Grade 0)
Seat #:____	Date:_____	Assignment:_____	Work Submitted: Yes ☐ No ☐ (Grade 0)
Seat #:____	Date:_____	Assignment:_____	Work Submitted: Yes ☐ No ☐ (Grade 0)
Seat #:____	Date:_____	Assignment:_____	Work Submitted: Yes ☐ No ☐ (Grade 0)
Seat #:____	Date:_____	Assignment:_____	Work Submitted: Yes ☐ No ☐ (Grade 0)
Seat #:____	Date:_____	Assignment:_____	Work Submitted: Yes ☐ No ☐ (Grade 0)
Seat #:____	Date:_____	Assignment:_____	Work Submitted: Yes ☐ No ☐ (Grade 0)
Seat #:____	Date:_____	Assignment:_____	Work Submitted: Yes ☐ No ☐ (Grade 0)
Seat #:____	Date:_____	Assignment:_____	Work Submitted: Yes ☐ No ☐ (Grade 0)
Seat #:____	Date:_____	Assignment:_____	Work Submitted: Yes ☐ No ☐ (Grade 0)
Seat #:____	Date:_____	Assignment:_____	Work Submitted: Yes ☐ No ☐ (Grade 0)
Seat #:____	Date:_____	Assignment:_____	Work Submitted: Yes ☐ No ☐ (Grade 0)
Seat #:____	Date:_____	Assignment:_____	Work Submitted: Yes ☐ No ☐ (Grade 0)
Seat #:____	Date:_____	Assignment:_____	Work Submitted: Yes ☐ No ☐ (Grade 0)
Seat #:____	Date:_____	Assignment:_____	Work Submitted: Yes ☐ No ☐ (Grade 0)
Seat #:____	Date:_____	Assignment:_____	Work Submitted: Yes ☐ No ☐ (Grade 0)
Seat #:____	Date:_____	Assignment:_____	Work Submitted: Yes ☐ No ☐ (Grade 0)
Seat #:____	Date:_____	Assignment:_____	Work Submitted: Yes ☐ No ☐ (Grade 0)
Seat #:____	Date:_____	Assignment:_____	Work Submitted: Yes ☐ No ☐ (Grade 0)
Seat #:____	Date:_____	Assignment:_____	Work Submitted: Yes ☐ No ☐ (Grade 0)

Student Late Work Filler

Students not submitting the required work within <u>today's class period</u> must:

- *Complete this <u>Student Late Work Filler</u> sheet and <u>Excuse Form (If applicable)</u>.*
- *Place filler sheet in student's mailbox slot within two minutes after teacher calls for assignment.*
- *Place the Excuse Form directly in your color-coded class folder.*
- If this process is not complete within the required time, student will lose an additional 10 points off his or her professionalism grade for not following instructions.

<u>Any late work not submitted within the allotted time will result in a grade of zero (0).</u> *See grading policy.*

Class Period	Student Name	Assignment	Due Date	-30 Points Date	"0" Grade Date

RJM-5b (DM)

Missing Work or Absent Student Filler

Reasons for missing work:
A= Absent student
M=Missing/Student did not turn in filler sheet and/or Excuse Blank Form

This section to be completed by teacher.

Seat #:	Date:	Missing Code:	Assignment	Work Submitted: Yes__ No__ (Grade 0)
Seat #:___	Date:____	Missing Code:___	Assignment_____	Work Submitted: Yes__ No__ (Grade 0)
Seat #:___	Date:____	Missing Code:___	Assignment_____	Work Submitted: Yes__ No__ (Grade 0)
Seat #:___	Date:____	Missing Code:___	Assignment_____	Work Submitted: Yes__ No__ (Grade 0)
Seat #:___	Date:____	Missing Code:___	Assignment_____	Work Submitted: Yes__ No__ (Grade 0)
Seat #:___	Date:____	Missing Code:___	Assignment_____	Work Submitted: Yes__ No__ (Grade 0)
Seat #:___	Date:____	Missing Code:___	Assignment_____	Work Submitted: Yes__ No__ (Grade 0)
Seat #:___	Date:____	Missing Code:___	Assignment_____	Work Submitted: Yes__ No__ (Grade 0)
Seat #:___	Date:____	Missing Code:___	Assignment_____	Work Submitted: Yes__ No__ (Grade 0)
Seat #:___	Date:____	Missing Code:___	Assignment_____	Work Submitted: Yes__ No__ (Grade 0)
Seat #:___	Date:____	Missing Code:___	Assignment_____	Work Submitted: Yes__ No__ (Grade 0)
Seat #:___	Date:____	Missing Code:___	Assignment_____	Work Submitted: Yes__ No__ (Grade 0)
Seat #:___	Date:____	Missing Code:___	Assignment_____	Work Submitted: Yes__ No__ (Grade 0)
Seat #:___	Date:____	Missing Code:___	Assignment_____	Work Submitted: Yes__ No__ (Grade 0)
Seat #:___	Date:____	Missing Code:___	Assignment_____	Work Submitted: Yes__ No__ (Grade 0)
Seat #:___	Date:____	Missing Code:___	Assignment_____	Work Submitted: Yes__ No__ (Grade 0)
Seat #:___	Date:____	Missing Code:___	Assignment_____	Work Submitted: Yes__ No__ (Grade 0)
Seat #:___	Date:____	Missing Code:___	Assignment_____	Work Submitted: Yes__ No__ (Grade 0)
Seat #:___	Date:____	Missing Code:___	Assignment_____	Work Submitted: Yes__ No__ (Grade 0)
Seat #:___	Date:____	Missing Code:___	Assignment_____	Work Submitted: Yes__ No__ (Grade 0)
Seat #:___	Date:____	Missing Code:___	Assignment_____	Work Submitted: Yes__ No__ (Grade 0)
Seat #:___	Date:____	Missing Code:___	Assignment_____	Work Submitted: Yes__ No__ (Grade 0)
Seat #:___	Date:____	Missing Code:___	Assignment_____	Work Submitted: Yes__ No__ (Grade 0)
Seat #:___	Date:____	Missing Code:___	Assignment_____	Work Submitted: Yes__ No__ (Grade 0)
Seat #:___	Date:____	Missing Code:___	Assignment_____	Work Submitted: Yes__ No__ (Grade 0)
Seat #:___	Date:____	Missing Code:___	Assignment_____	Work Submitted: Yes__ No__ (Grade 0)
Seat #:___	Date:____	Missing Code:___	Assignment_____	Work Submitted: Yes__ No__ (Grade 0)

Tardy Log (Students in seats 1-30)

This log book will be used to determine your conduct grade and your evaluation at the end of the semester or rotation, and it will be used for recommendations etc. and be sent to the nurse or office if necessary. Please print your name legibly next to your seat number (if not done already). When a violation occurs, write the date, your initials, and the violation code below the tardy number that corresponds to your violation.

Offense	Tardy Codes
FIRST Tardy	W
SECOND Tardy	D
THIRD Tardy	D1
FOURTH Tardy	D2
FIFTH Tardy	DP
SIXTH Tardy (or more)	DU

Consequence (With each tardy, student must sign tardy log.)
- Warning or other actions by the teacher
- ½ hour of detention after school (See school policy for days and times.)
- 1 hour of detention after school and "S" (See school policy for days and times.)
- 2 hours of detention after school (See school policy for days and times.)
- Conduct of "P" in class and student will be placed on probation.
- Student assigned to SAC (off campus). Office conduct of "U"
- End of the year exit conference with student and parent

Seat NO.	Student Name Please Print Legibly!	1st Tardy Good Rating			2nd Tardy Average Rating			3rd Tardy - Below Average Rating - "S" in Conduct			4th Tardy - Poor Rating "S" in Conduct			5th Tardy - Poor Rating "P" Probation			6th Tardy - Terrible Rating - Office Visit		
		Date	Student Initial	Tardy Code	Date	Student Initials	Tardy Code	Date	Student Initials	Tardy Code	Date	Student Initials	Tardy Code	Date	Student Initials	Tardy Code	Date	Student Initials	Tardy Code
1																			
2																			
3																			
4																			
5																			
6																			
7																			
8																			
9																			
10																			
11																			
12																			
13																			
14																			
15																			
16																			
17																			
18																			
19																			
20																			
21																			
22																			
23																			
24																			
25																			
26																			
27																			
28																			
29																			
30																			

Tardy Log (Students in seats 31-60)

This log book will be used to determine your conduct grade and your evaluation at the end of the semester or rotation, and it will be used for recommendations etc. and be sent to the nurse or office if necessary. Please print your name legibly next to your seat number (if not done already). When a violation occurs, write the date, your initials, and the violation code below the tardy number that corresponds to your violation.

Offense	Tardy Codes	Consequence (With each tardy, student must sign tardy log.)
FIRST Tardy	W	Warning or other actions by the teacher
SECOND Tardy	D	½ hour of detention after school (See school policy for days and times.)
THIRD Tardy	D1	1 hour of detention after school and "S" (See school policy for days and times.)
FOURTH Tardy	D2	2 hours of detention after school (See school policy for days and times.)
FIFTH Tardy	DP	Conduct of "P" in class and student will be placed on probation
SIXTH Tardy (or more)	DU	Student assigned to SAC (off campus). Office conduct of "U" End of the year exit conference with student and parent

Seat NO.	Student Name Please Print Legibly!!	1st Tardy Good Rating			2nd Tardy Average Rating			3rd Tardy-Below Average Rating – "S" in Conduct			4th Tardy - Poor Rating "S" in Conduct			5th Tardy - Poor Rating "P" Probation			6th Tardy - Terrible Rating - Office Visit		
		Date	Student Initial	Tardy Code	Date	Student Initials	Tardy Code	Date	Student Initials	Tardy Code	Date	Student Initials	Tardy Code	Date	Student Initials	Tardy Code	Date	Student Initials	Tardy Code
31																			
32																			
33																			
34																			
35																			
36																			
37																			
38																			
39																			
40																			
41																			
42																			
43																			
44																			
45																			
46																			
47																			
48																			
49																			
50																			
51																			
52																			
53																			
54																			
55																			
56																			
57																			
58																			
59																			
60																			

Detention Log Sheet

Student Name	Seat #	Class Period	Date Detention Served	Time In	Time Out	Total Minutes	Conduct Restored √	Comments

RMJ-8

Conduct Log (Students in seats 1-30)

This log book will be used to determine your conduct grade and your evaluation at the end of the semester or rotation, and it will be used for recommendations etc. and be sent to the nurse or office if necessary. Please print your name legibly next to your seat number (if not done already). When a violation occurs, write the date, your initials, and the violation code below that which corresponds to your violation.

Violation Codes:

a. Failure to be in assigned seat
b. Use of bad language
c. Chewing gum, eating, or drinking in class
d. Applying makeup or combing hair in class
e. Sleeping in class or putting your head down or feet up on desk
f. Talking while test is in progress
g. Writing or passing notes while teacher is lecturing
h. Talking while teacher is lecturing or others are presenting
i. Horse playing or game playing
j. Talking too much or too loud
k. Disrespecting instructor or others
l. Failure to return required parent signature documents
m. Other offense (See Student Handbook.)

Seat NO.	Student Name Please Print Legibly!	1st Violation Good Rating			2nd Violation Average Rating			3rd Violation - Below Avg. Rating - "S" in Conduct			4th Violation - Poor Rating - "S" in Conduct			5th Violation - Poor Rating - "P" Probation			6th Violation - Terrible Rating - Office Visit			Cycle	Cycle	Cycle
		Date	Student Initial	Code	Date	Student Initials	Code	Date	Student Initial	Code	Date	Student Initials	Code	Date	Student Initials	Code	Date	Student Initials	Code	Grade	Grade	Grade
1																						
2																						
3																						
4																						
5																						
6																						
7																						
8																						
9																						
10																						
11																						
12																						
13																						
14																						
15																						
16																						
17																						
18																						
19																						
20																						
21																						
22																						
23																						
24																						
25																						
26																						
27																						
28																						
29																						
30																						

Conduct Log (Students in seats 31-60)

This log book will be used to determine your conduct grade and your evaluation at the end of the semester or rotation, and it will be used for recommendations etc. and be sent to the nurse or office if necessary. Please print your name legibly next to your seat number (if not done already). When a violation occurs, write the date, your initials, and the violation code below that which corresponds to your violation.

Violation Codes:

a. Failure to be in assigned seat
b. Use of bad language
c. Chewing gum, eating, or drinking in class
d. Applying makeup or combing hair in class
e. Sleeping in class or putting your head down or feet up on desk
f. Talking while test is in progress
g. Writing or passing notes while teacher is lecturing
h. Talking while teacher is lecturing or others are presenting
i. Horse playing or game playing
j. Talking too much or too loud
k. Disrespecting instructor or others
l. Failure to return required parent signature documents
m. Other offense (See Student Handbook.)

Seat NO.	Student Name Please Print Legibly!	1st Violation Good Rating			2nd Violation Average Rating			3rd Violation - Below Avg. Rating - "S" in Conduct			4th Violation - Poor Rating - "S" in Conduct			5th Violation - Poor Rating - "P" Probation			6th Violation- Terrible Rating - Office Visit			Cycle	Cycle	Cycle
		Date	Student Initial	Code	Date	Student Initials	Code	Date	Student Initial	Code	Date	Student Initials	Code	Date	Student Initials	Code	Date	Student Initials	Code	Grade	Grade	Grade
31																						
32																						
33																						
34																						
35																						
36																						
37																						
38																						
39																						
40																						
41																						
42																						
43																						
44																						
45																						
46																						
47																						
48																						
49																						
50																						
51																						
52																						
53																						
54																						
55																						
56																						
57																						
58																						
59																						
60																						

Professionalism Log (Students in seats 1-30)

This log book will be used to determine your professionalism grade and your evaluation at the end of the semester or rotation, and it will be used for recommendations etc.

Please print your name legibly next to your seat number (if not done already). When a violation occurs, write the date, your initials, and the violation code below that which corresponds to your violation.

Safety Violations
1. Unauthorized or improper handling of instruments or equipment or supplies.
2. Failure to keep backpacks purses or nonessential items off desk and isles *at all times*.
3. Failure to follow safety instructions given by teacher including proper dress attire (i.e. Lab coat).
4. Failure to replace equipment and supplies in the designated areas.
5. Failure to clean up immediate surroundings and work areas.
6. Failure to disinfect all contaminated areas.

Professionalism Codes

General Violations
7. Failure to bring books and notebooks to class on a daily basis.
8. Failure to take required notes.
9. Failure to participate in class activities.
10. Failure to follow teachers' instructions on assignments (i.e. working on outside assignments, reading novels, etc).

Seat NO.	Student Name Please Print Legibly!	1st Violation Good Rating			2nd Violation Average Rating			3rd Violation Below Average Rating			4th Violation Poor Rating			5th Violation Terrible Rating		
		Date	Student Initials	Volition Code	Date	Student Initials	Volition Code	Date	Student Initials	Volition Code	Date	Student Initials	Volition Code	Date	Student Initials	Volition Code
1																
2																
3																
4																
5																
6																
7																
8																
9																
10																
11																
12																
13																
14																
15																
16																
17																
18																
19																
20																
21																
22																
23																
24																
25																
26																
27																
28																
29																
30																

Professionalism Log (Students in seats 31-60)

This log book will be used to determine your professionalism grade and evaluation at the end of the semester or rotation, and it will be used for recommendations etc. Please print legibly your name next to your seat number (if not done already). When a violation occurs, write the date, your initials, and the violation code below which corresponds to your violation.

Violations Codes

1. _____
2. _____
3. _____
4. _____
5. _____

Professionalism Codes

6. _____
7. _____
8. _____
9. _____
10. _____

Seat NO.	Student Name Please Print Legibly!!	1st Violation Good Rating			2nd Violation Average Rating			3rd Violation Below Average Rating			4th Violation Poor rating			5th Violation Terrible Rating		
		Date	Student Initials	Volition Code	Date	Student Initials	Volition Code	Date	Student Initials	Volition Code	Date	Student Initials	Volition Code	Date	Student Initials	Volition Code
31																
32																
33																
34																
35																
36																
37																
38																
39																
40																
41																
42																
43																
44																
45																
46																
47																
48																
49																
50																
51																
52																
53																
54																
55																
56																
57																
58																
59																
60																

Professionalism Log For Cycle(s) _____

This log book will be used to determine your professionalism grade at the end of each cycle and your evaluations at the end of year or rotation. It will be used for recommendations etc. Please print your name legibly next to your seat number (if not done already). When a violation occurs, write the date, your initials, and the violation code below that which corresponds to your violation.

Safety Violations

1. Unauthorized or improper handling of instruments or equipment or supplies
2. Failure to keep backpacks, purses, or nonessential items off desk and in isles at *all times*
3. Failure to follow safety instructions given by teacher, including proper dress attire (i.e. lab coat)
4. Failure to replace equipment and supplies in the designated areas
5. Failure to clean up immediate surroundings and work areas
6. Failure to disinfect all contaminated areas

General Violations

7. Failure to bring books and notebooks to class on a daily basis
8. Failure to take required notes
9. Failure to participate in class activities
10. Failure to follow teacher's instructions on assignments (i.e., working on outside assignments, reading novels, etc.)

Professionalism Codes

Seat NO.	Student Name Please Print Legibly!	1st Violation Good Rating			2nd Violation Average Rating			3rd Violation Below Average Rating			4th Violation Poor Rating			5th Violation Terrible Rating			Cycle: Grade:	Cycle: Grade:	Cycle: Grade:
		Date	Student Initials	Volition Code	Date	Student Initials	Volition Code	Date	Student Initials	Volition Code	Date	Student Initials	Volition Code	Date	Student Initials	Volition Code			
1																			
2																			
3																			
4																			
5																			
6																			
7																			
8																			
9																			
10																			
11																			
12																			
13																			
14																			
15																			
16																			
17																			
18																			
19																			
20																			
21																			
22																			
23																			
24																			
25																			
26																			
27																			
28																			
29																			
30																			

Professionalism Log (Students in seats 31-60) For Cycle(s) _____

This log book will be used to determine your professionalism grade at the end of each cycle and your evaluations at the end of year or rotation. It will be used for recommendations etc. Please print your name legibly next to your seat number (if not done already). When a violation occurs, write the date, your initials, and the violation code below that which corresponds to your violation.

Safety Violations
1. Unauthorized or improper handling of instruments or equipment or supplies
2. Failure to keep backpacks, purses, or nonessential items off desk and in isles at *all times*
3. Failure to follow safety instructions given by teacher, including proper dress attire (i.e. lab coat)
4. Failure to replace equipment and supplies in the designated areas
5. Failure to clean up immediate surroundings and work areas
6. Failure to disinfect all contaminated areas

General Violations
7. Failure to bring books and notebooks to class on a daily basis
8. Failure to take required notes
9. Failure to participate in class activities
10. Failure to follow teacher's instructions on assignments (i.e., working on outside assignments, reading novels, etc.)

Professionalism Codes

Seat NO.	Student Name Please Print Legibly!	1st Violation Good Rating			2nd Violation Average Rating			3rd Violation Below Average Rating			4th Violation Poor Rating			5th Violation Terrible Rating			Cycle: Grade:	Cycle: Grade:	Cycle: Grade:
		Date	Student Initials	Volition Code	Date	Student Initials	Volition Code	Date	Student Initials	Volition Code	Date	Student Initials	Volition Code	Date	Student Initials	Volition Code			
31																			
32																			
33																			
34																			
35																			
36																			
37																			
38																			
39																			
40																			
41																			
42																			
43																			
44																			
45																			
46																			
47																			
48																			
49																			
50																			
51																			
52																			
53																			
54																			
55																			
56																			
57																			
58																			
59																			
60																			

Temporary Log Sheet

Student Name	Seat #	Date	Class Period	Tardy Code	Prof Code	Conduct Code			Transferred to Log

RMJ-11

Extra Credit Log

Class Period(s) _____ Cycle _____ Year _____

Student's Seat No.	Student's Name															Extra Credit Total
1																
2																
3																
4																
5																
6																
7																
8																
9																
10																
11																
12																
13																
14																
15																
16																
17																
18																
19																
20																
21																
22																
23																
24																
25																
26																
27																
28																
29																
30																
31																
32																
33																
34																
35																
36																

RMJ-12

Student Sign out Log

Student Name	Date	Reason for being excused from class:	Pass #	Time Excused	Time Returned

Copies of this log may be sent to the office, counselor or nurse if necessary.

RMJ-13

Student Hall Pass

Teacher

- Please be sure to sign out and date pass.
- Bring slip to instructor for initials.
- Sign back in class; put pass back.
- File hall pass in seat number order.

Student's Name   Seat No.
_____   _____

Date _____   Teacher's Initials _____
Date _____   Teacher's Initials _____
Date _____   Teacher's Initials _____
Date _____   Teacher's Initials _____
Date _____   Teacher's Initials _____
Date _____   Teacher's Initials _____

After using all six passes, you must take a tardy to leave class. Make sure it is necessary. Thanks!

Student Hall Pass

Teacher

- Please be sure to sign out and date pass.
- Bring slip to instructor for initials.
- Sign back in class; put pass back.
- File hall pass in seat number order.

Student's Name   Seat No.
_____   _____

Date _____   Teacher's Initials _____
Date _____   Teacher's Initials _____
Date _____   Teacher's Initials _____
Date _____   Teacher's Initials _____
Date _____   Teacher's Initials _____
Date _____   Teacher's Initials _____

After using all six passes, you must take a tardy to leave class. Make sure it is necessary. Thanks!

Student Hall Pass

Teacher

- Please be sure to sign out and date pass.
- Bring slip to instructor for initials.
- Sign back in class; put pass back.
- File hall pass in seat number order.

Student's Name   Seat No.
_____   _____

Date _____   Teacher's Initials _____
Date _____   Teacher's Initials _____
Date _____   Teacher's Initials _____
Date _____   Teacher's Initials _____
Date _____   Teacher's Initials _____
Date _____   Teacher's Initials _____

After using all six passes, you must take a tardy to leave class. Make sure it is necessary. Thanks!

Student Hall Pass

Teacher

- Please be sure to sign out and date pass.
- Bring slip to instructor for initials.
- Sign back in class; put pass back.
- File hall pass in seat number order.

Student's Name   Seat No.
_____   _____

Date _____   Teacher's Initials _____
Date _____   Teacher's Initials _____
Date _____   Teacher's Initials _____
Date _____   Teacher's Initials _____
Date _____   Teacher's Initials _____
Date _____   Teacher's Initials _____

After using all six passes, you must take a tardy to leave class. Make sure it is necessary. Thanks!

Student Sign-In Log

Student Name	Date	Reason for visit:	Excused From:	Time IN	Time OUT

Please fill out this form. Detach it from the packet, and have the student return it to me the next time he/she attends this class.

Student/Parent Grading Policy Signature Form
Teacher Copy

I have read and understand the grading policies of the Health Science Program. *In addition, DeBakey High School students who are tardy will not be allowed in class without a permit from the office.*

I understand that I need to stay on task with homework, class assignments, and my health science notes every night in order to be successful and that I may be required to take an unscheduled quiz at any time. I also understand that my class can be videotaped for educational purposes or for the promotion of the school.

To be completed by student

_____ _____ ___/___/___
Printed Name of Student   Student's Signature   Date Signed

To be completed by Parent/Guardian

Parent/Guardian printed name: _____

Parent/Guardian preferred contact number: _____

Parent/Guardian email address: _____

Problems and Disabilities: Please inform instructor and student's counselor of any problems, temporary or long-term, that might interfere with student's ability to participate fully in class so that the teacher/counselor can make accommodations to assist the student in coursework while the student is coping with extra problems. If none, write N/A in the first line.

_____
_____
_____
_____
_____

Parent/Guardian Signature: _____
_____/_____/_____
Date Signed by Parent/Guardian

RMJ-b

PERSONAL DATA AND EVALUATION SHEET

NAME _____ SEAT # _____ Period(s) _____ Cycle/Year _____

ADDRESS _____ Zip Code _____

HOMEROOM TEACHER _____ STUDENT ID # _____

	Mother	Father

Mother
- Name: _____
- Occupation: _____
- Work Contact No.: _____
- Home Contact No.: _____
- Cell Phone No.: _____

Father
- Name: _____
- Occupation: _____
- Work Contact No.: _____
- Home Contact No.: _____
- Cell Phone No.: _____

BIRTH DATE _____ AGE _____ RACE (Circle one):   White   Black   Hispanic   Asian   American Indian

PRIMARY CAREER CHOICE _____ *ALTERNATE* CAREER CHOICES:
1) _____   2) _____   3) _____

CLASS SCHEDULE (PRINT IN PENCIL ONLY!!!)

PERIOD	SUBJECT	ROOM	INSTRUCTOR	REMARKS OR CHANGES
1				
2				
3				
4				
5				
6				
7				
8				

Student Portfolio Evaluation (Optional)

Name _____ Subject _____ Year _____

INSTRUCTOR EVALUATION OF STUDENT TO USE FOR STUDENT RECONMENDATIONS

EVALUATIONS CATEGORIES	POOR RECORD	BELOW AVERAGE	AVERAGE RECORD	GOOD RECORD	EXCELLENT RECORD
ATTENDANCE					
PUNCTUALITY					
CONDUCT					
PROFESSIONALISM					
GRADES					
PARTICIPATION SELF-MOTIVATED					
FOLLOWING INSTRUCTIONS					
LAB DUTIES AND RESPONSIBILITIES					
TEAMWORK					
OVERALL CLASS ATTITUDE					

WOULD INSTRUCTOR HIRE THIS STUDENT AS AN ASSISTANT?   YES   NO   MAYBE

RMJ-17

INSTRUCTOR EVALUATION CRITERIA OF STUDENT
(To be sent along with letters of recommendations)

EVALUATIONS CATEGORIES	POOR RECORD	BELOW AVERAGE	AVERAGE RECORD	GOOD RECORD	EXCELLENT RECORD
ATTENDANCE	Absent 4+ days	Absent 3 days	Absent 2 days	Absent 1 day	Absent 0 days
PUNCTUALITY	Tardy 4+ times	Tardy 3 times	Tardy 2 times	Tardy 1 time	Tardy 0 times
CONDUCT	4+ Offenses	3 Offenses	2 Offenses	1 Offense	0 Offenses
PROFESSIONALISM	4+ Offenses	3 Offenses	2 Offenses	1 Offense	0 Offenses
GRADES	< 70	70 - 74	75 - 79	80 - 89	90 - 100
PARTICIPATION SELF-MOTOVATED	Almost never	Occasional	Sometimes	Most of the time	Always
FOLLOWING INSTRUCTIONS	Almost never	Occasional	Sometimes	Most of the time	Always
LAB DUTIES AND RESPONSIBILITIES	Almost never	Occasional	Sometimes	Most of the time	Always
TEAMWORK	Does not get along with peers	Gets along with few peers	Gets along with avg. # of peers	Gets along with majority of peers	Gets along with almost all peers
OVERALL CLASS ATTITUDE	Always complaining, etc.	Frequent complaining, etc.	Sometimes complaining, etc.	Infrequent complaining, etc.	Almost never complaining, etc.

WOULD INSTRUCTOR HIRE THIS STUDENT AS AN ASSISTANT?   YES   NO   MAYBE

RMJ-17

DUTIES AND RESPONSIBILITIES Sign Up Sheet: Class Period(s) __ Class Size___

All students enrolled in career and technology classes will be assigned one of the following duties. Most students are aware of the accomplishments and leadership abilities of their classmates; therefore elections will be held for the same positions so that the most qualified students will hold these positions. Students will be asked to volunteer for the remaining positions; but, please remember that **all** students will be assigned only **one** duty. Performance of duties is part of students' official course evaluations (see evaluation criteria) and will be counted for a daily grade. (Space for seat #) Space for student name i.e., (5) John Doe

*Supervisor (1 student) (*student elected using parliamentary procedure when time is available) (__)_____
- takes daily attendance (optional) in student log book, gives oral report to teacher, and places written log book report in teacher's hand.
- reads script in supervisor log book which reminds students about storing backpacks, checking work area for trash, spitting out gum, etc.
- performs guest relations when assistant supervisor is absent or along with the assistant if you wish
- fills positions when no floater(s) is available and serves as timekeeper for the class

*Assistant Supervisor(s) / Public Relations Officer(s) (2 students) (__)_____ (__)_____
- read daily assignment calendar (current day and next class day).
- check the student baskets daily for announcements; read short announcements at the beginning of class after all assignments are turned in. Read long announcements first, and then summarize to the class. Also, delegate any handouts to teacher assistant to issue to class
- perform guest relations (greet visitors at the door; introduce self, point out teacher, explain the program, and explain what the class is presently doing.)
- make sure students leave workstation in a neat and orderly fashion by going around the room a minute before the dismissal bell to remind students to push in chairs and pick up trash.

*Safety Officer & Teachers Assistants (TA) (2) (__)_____ (__)_____
- issue handouts and file leftover handouts in appropriate place
- perform various tasks assigned by teacher
- perform duties of safety officer for fire drills and when a student gets a minor injury. For fire drills, one TA will lead students to the designated area. The other TA will be at the end of the line helping to guide students to the appropriate place, and both TAs will help students get in seat order for roll call during the drill.

*Homework Helper & Teachers Assistants (TA) (1-2) (__)_____ (__)_____
- issue handouts and file leftover handouts in appropriate place
- Help students who do not understand the assignment over the phone or computer. Student must provide students with phone number and e-mail address
- Students must check e-mail daily and respond by 8 p.m. nightly.

*Board Monitor & Teachers Assistants (TA) (1-2) (__)_____ (__)_____
- write on board when necessary and erases board when necessary
- issue handouts and file leftover handouts in appropriate place
- perform various tasks assigned by teacher

*Scranton Technician & Teacher Assistant (1-2) (__)_____ (__)_____
- pass out scantron for all test and quizzes
- issue handouts and file leftover handouts in appropriate place
- perform various tasks assigned by teacher

Electronic Technician (1-2) (__)_____ (__)_____
- set up TV for VHS or DVD movies, play music CDs at the beginning of each class, etc, and controls the remote control when necessary.
- start music instrumental only DVD at the beginning of each class while students are entering class
- turns on projector daily for instructions after quiz and lab PowerPoints

Supply Technician (1-2) (__)_____ (__)_____
- make sure all students have pencil, paper, etc., at the beginning of class
- pass out scratch paper needed or lab data daily before each lab
- empty pencil sharpener and refill stapler

Mailbox Technician (1-2) (__)_____ (__)_____
- collect items out of mailbox slots and bring to teacher
- collect excuse blank forms and files in student folders

Sink and/or Countertop Managers (2) (__)_____ (__)_____
- replenished soap, paper towels, hand sanitizer (Stock is in storeroom.)
- make sure sink/desk are left cleaned at the end of the period by passing out sanitizing wipes to students
- put paper towel work mats on each station when needed for labs, projects, etc.

Equipment & Desk Managers (2-4) (__)_____ (__)_____ (__)_____ (__)_____
- gather supplies for labs
- replace equipment after each use
- straighten out desk/tables in proper rows/position, making sure desk/tables are not too close to other desk/tables

**Reagent, Glassware & Pipette Technicians (1-2) (__)_____ (__)_____
- make and issue reagents needed for labs
- maintain distilled water supply under sink in storeroom
- obtain glassware, wash, rinse, and dry glassware when instructed
- (The first class to use glassware will obtain it. The last class to use it will wash it.)

Lab Floaters (1-3) (__)_____ (__)_____ (__)_____
- fill position(s) when students are absent and helps when there is an overload for one function

*student elected using parliamentary procedure when time is available
***Duties apply to lab classes only.*

Daily Responsibility Log Sheet: Period ___

Dates of duties performed. Please check daily!

Seat#	First Name	Duty Title																													
1																															
2																															
3																															
4																															
5																															
6																															
7																															
8																															
9																															
10																															
11																															
12																															
13																															
14																															
15																															
16																															
17																															
18																															
19																															
20																															
21																															
22																															
23																															
24																															
25																															
26																															
27																															
28																															
29																															
30																															

Assignment Calendar: Course _____ Cycle _____ Year _____

	Monday	Tuesday	Wednesday	Thursday	Friday
	Date:	Date:	Date:	Date:	Date:
Week 1					
	Date:	Date:	Date:	Date:	Date:
Week 2					
	Date:	Date:	Date:	Date:	Date:
Week 3					
	Date:	Date:	Date:	Date:	Date:
Week 4					
	Date:	Date:	Date:	Date:	Date:
Week 5					
	Date:	Date:	Date:	Date:	Date:
Week 6					

RMJ-22

Daily Clean Up Log

Class Period(s) _____ Cycle _____ Year _____

Use only if trash needs to be recorded. Use the next column available. Put the date and a brief description of trash (i.e., can, paper, bag). Put "L" if it is a lost or found item.

Seat #	Date	Date	Date	Date	Date	Date	Date	Date	Date	Date	Date	Date	Date	Date	Date
1															
2															
3															
4															
5															
6															
7															
8															
9															
10															
11															
12															
13															
14															
15															
16															
17															
18															
19															
20															
21															
22															
23															
24															
25															
26															
27															
28															
29															
30															
31															
32															

RMJ-23

Course Name: _____ **GRADE SHEET**

Cycle _____

Name _____ Student ID# _____ Seat# _____ Approved __

____% **Daily Grades or** _____

Date	Subject	Grade
Avg. Daily Grade	X. _____	Raw Score

____% **Major Grades or** _____

Date	Subject	Grade
Avg. Major Grade	X. _____	Raw Score

____% **Professionalism or** _____

Date	Subject	Grade
Avg. Prof Grade	X. _____	Raw Score

Raw Score Total

Daily Grade Raw Score	
Major Raw Score	
Prof Raw Score	
Six Weeks Grade	

Grade Scale

90-100 …………………..A
80-89 …………………..B
75-79 …………………..C
70-74 …………………..D
0-69 …………………..F

To Be Completed By Teacher	Number Grade	Letter Grade
Final Six Week Grade		
Conduct Grade		
Total Times Absent	Excused _____	Unexcused _____

RMJ-24

Name _____ Seat# _____
Teacher _____
Subject _____ Period _____
Date _____

Notebook Grade Sheet

Cycle 4

Subject	Total Points	Student Self Check√	Student Points Lost	Teacher Check√	Teacher Points Lost
Proper Notebook	5				
Cover Sheet	1				
Title Page Completed	1				
Daily Assignment Sheet Completed	5				
Orientation Material	5				
Grade Sheet	5				
Neatness with Dividers with Pencil Pouch & Supplies	10				
Decision-Making Written Notes	5				
Decision-Making Multi-Activity Worksheet	5				
Medical Terminology Information Sheet 1 & 2	1				
Basic Anatomy & Physiology Notes	1				
MT Lesson 1 Homework (2 Lessons 3 points each)	6				
MT Lesson 2 Homework (2 Lessons 3 points each)	6				
MT Lesson 3 Homework (2 Lessons 3 points each)	6				
MT Lesson 4 Homework (2 Lessons 3 points each)	6				
MT Lesson 5 Homework (2 Lessons 3 points each)	6				
Understanding Yourself Written Notes	5				
Understanding Yourself Multi-Activity Worksheet 1	5				
Understanding Yourself Multi-Activity Worksheet 2	5				
Understanding Yourself Multi-Activity Worksheet 3	5				
Understanding Yourself Multi-Activity Worksheet 4	5				
Mission Statement	1				
Total Points	100 Total Points		Total Lost Points	Teacher Bonus Points	Total Lost Points
Notebook Grade			Student Self Grade	Teacher Subtotal	Student Final Grade

RMJ-25

Course Name:_____

Lesson Plan Assignment Calendar
Cycle _____

Monday	Tuesday	Wednesday	Thursday	Friday
Date:____	Date:____	Date:____	Date:____	Date:____
Lesson Plan ____	Lesson Plan ____	Lesson Plan ____	Lesson Plan ____	Lesson Plan ____
Date:____	Date:____	Date:____	Date:____	Date:____
Lesson Plan ____	Lesson Plan ____	Lesson Plan ____	Lesson Plan ____	Lesson Plan ____
Date:____	Date:____	Date:____	Date:____	Date:____
Lesson Plan ____	Lesson Plan ____	Lesson Plan ____	Lesson Plan ____	Lesson Plan ____
Date:____	Date:____	Date:____	Date:____	Date:____
Lesson Plan ____	Lesson Plan ____	Lesson Plan ____	Lesson Plan ____	Lesson Plan ____
Date:____	Date:____	Date:____	Date:____	Date:____
Lesson Plan ____	Lesson Plan ____	Lesson Plan ____	Lesson Plan ____	Lesson Plan ____
Date:____	Date:____	Date:____	Date:____	Date:____
Lesson Plan ____	Lesson Plan ____	Lesson Plan ____	Lesson Plan ____	Lesson Plan ____
Date:____	Date:____	Date:____	Date:____	Date:____
Lesson Plan ____	Lesson Plan ____	Lesson Plan ____	Lesson Plan ____	Lesson Plan ____

Note: This is a tentative schedule. Necessary changes will be made depending upon other school activities, and those changes will be announced in class.

Lesson Plan

Instructor: _____ School _____
Course _____ Lesson Plan Number _____
Subject _____ A & B Days (Plan may expand more than one period.)
Unit _____ Section _____ Other _____

OBJECTIVE

THE STUDENT WILL:
- ☐ _____
- ☐ _____
- ☐ _____
- ☐ _____
- ☐ _____

PREPARATION

Student Resources: _____
_____

Instructional Aid: _____
_____

Materials: _____
_____

PRESENTATION

_____
_____
_____
_____

APPLICATIONS

Related Activities:
_____
_____
_____

Misc. Activities:
_____
_____

ASSESSMENT

_____

RMJ-27

Student Summons Page
Assistant Supervisor, please say,

"The students in the following seat numbers need to come forward at this time and see our instructor."

Give this sheet to the instructor as a reminder of why the student was summoned. Ignore seat numbers crossed out; actions are completed.

Seat #___: ☐ code ___ violation; ☐ late work; ☐ absent work; other: _____

Seat #___: ☐ code ___ violation; ☐ late work; ☐ absent work; other: _____

Seat #___: ☐ code ___ violation; ☐ late work; ☐ absent work; other: _____

Seat #___: ☐ code ___ violation; ☐ late work; ☐ absent work; other: _____

Seat #___: ☐ code ___ violation; ☐ late work; ☐ absent work; other: _____

Seat #___: ☐ code ___ violation; ☐ late work; ☐ absent work; other: _____

Seat #___: ☐ code ___ violation; ☐ late work; ☐ absent work; other: _____

Seat #___: ☐ code ___ violation; ☐ late work; ☐ absent work; other: _____

Seat #___: ☐ code ___ violation; ☐ late work; ☐ absent work; other: _____

Seat #___: ☐ code ___ violation; ☐ late work; ☐ absent work; other: _____

Seat #___: ☐ code ___ violation; ☐ late work; ☐ absent work; other: _____

Seat #___: ☐ code ___ violation; ☐ late work; ☐ absent work; other: _____

Seat #___: ☐ code ___ violation; ☐ late work; ☐ absent work; other: _____

Seat #___: ☐ code ___ violation; ☐ late work; ☐ absent work; other: _____

Seat #___: ☐ code ___ violation; ☐ late work; ☐ absent work; other: _____

Seat #___: ☐ code ___ violation; ☐ late work; ☐ absent work; other: _____

Seat #___: ☐ code ___ violation; ☐ late work; ☐ absent work; other: _____

Seat #___: ☐ code ___ violation; ☐ late work; ☐ absent work; other: _____

Seat #___: ☐ code ___ violation; ☐ late work; ☐ absent work; other: _____

Seat #___: ☐ code ___ violation; ☐ late work; ☐ absent work; other: _____

Seat #___: ☐ code ___ violation; ☐ late work; ☐ absent work; other: _____

Seat #___: ☐ code ___ violation; ☐ late work; ☐ absent work; other: _____

Seat #___: ☐ code ___ violation; ☐ late work; ☐ absent work; other: _____

BROKEN ITEMS LOG

Student Name and Seat #	Date	Description of item broken	Retail cost	Student's cost	Date and Amt. Pd.

"Typo" Log

Period ___ Document Type (i.e., Microbiology Notes)_____

Student Name	Seat #	"Typo" Item	Item # or Location	Wrong word, grammar, etc.	Right word, grammar, etc.

RMJ-30

Student Permit

Date _____ Time _____

Student's Name _____

- ☐ Please allow student to attend my _____ class.
- ☐ Please allow student to report to lunch late.
- ☐ Please allow student to: _____
- ☐ Please allow student to use library.
- ☐ Please allow student to exit building.
- Other _____

_____
Signature of adult initiating permit.

_____
Receiving teacher approval to accept student

Student Permit

Date _____ Time _____

Student's Name _____

- ☐ Please allow student to attend my _____ class.
- ☐ Please allow student to report to lunch late.
- ☐ Please allow student to: _____
- ☐ Please allow student to use library.
- ☐ Please allow student to exit building.
- Other _____

_____
Signature of adult initiating permit.

_____
Receiving teacher approval to accept student

Student Permit

Date _____ Time _____

Student's Name _____

- ☐ Please allow student to attend my _____ class.
- ☐ Please allow student to report to lunch late.
- ☐ Please allow student to: _____
- ☐ Please allow student to use library.
- ☐ Please allow student to exit building.
- Other _____

_____
Signature of adult initiating permit.

_____
Receiving teacher approval to accept student

Student Permit

Date _____ Time _____

Student's Name _____

- ☐ Please allow student to attend my _____ class.
- ☐ Please allow student to report to lunch late.
- ☐ Please allow student to: _____
- ☐ Please allow student to use library.
- ☐ Please allow student to exit building.
- Other _____

_____
Signature of adult initiating permit.

_____
Receiving teacher approval to accept student

Student Permit

Date _____ Time _____

Student's Name _____

- ☐ Please allow student to attend my _____ class.
- ☐ Please allow student to report to lunch late.
- ☐ Please allow student to: _____
- ☐ Please allow student to use library.
- ☐ Please allow student to exit building.
- Other _____

_____
Signature of adult initiating permit.

_____
Receiving teacher approval to accept student

Student Permit

Date _____ Time _____

Student's Name _____

- ☐ Please allow student to attend my _____ class.
- ☐ Please allow student to report to lunch late.
- ☐ Please allow student to: _____
- ☐ Please allow student to use library.
- ☐ Please allow student to exit building.
- Other _____

_____
Signature of adult initiating permit.

_____
Receiving teacher approval to accept student

School Name

_____

School Address

_____

_____

School Phone Number

_____

Subject _____

Instructor _____

Conference Period_____ Time_____ Day_____

Student Name:_____ Student Seat No._____

Period(s)_____ School Year_____

Student's Class Duty or Responsibility:_____

The duties of all students are to stay on task, study daily, be and courteous to others. Write a brief description of the duties that you were assigned or elected below.

Description of Duties and Responsibilities

_____
_____
_____
_____
_____

This Notebook Belongs to:

Student Name: _____   Student Seat No._____

School Name

_____

School Address

_____
_____

School Phone Number

_____

Subject_____

Instructor_____

Period(s)_____   School Year_____

Table of Content for Tabs

Color Code or Number Code	Subsections of notebook

STUDENTS' LOG BOOK

Period(s)_____

Use for:
- **SIGNING OUT OF CLASS***
- **TARDIES**
- **PROFESSIONALISM**
- **CONDUCT**
- **EXTRA CREDIT**

*Sign-out sheet may be posted in another location. (See teacher.)

Cut for Spine of binder

STUDENTS' LOG BOOK Period(s)_____

RMJ-34

Medical Laboratory Assisting Course Overview

This nine-week course includes the below sections. (Depending on the student's class schedule, the nine-week rotaion can be during the 1st semester or the 2nd semester.)

Introduction to lab, safety, and lab skills (2 weeks)	Clinical Immunology/Serology (1week)
Urinalysis (1 weeks)	Microbiology (3 weeks)
Hematology (2 weeks)	Clinical Chemistry (2 Days)

Grading Policy
Students will receive a separate grading policy document for this rotation. Students are expected to follow grading policy provided by instructor, and students and parents must sign a from stating they have reviewed the grading policy.

Course Goals Are:
- To obtain sufficient information, observation, and practical experience of a wide range of lab procedures and classroom responsibilities that will prepare students for entry-level employment and higher education in the health profession
- To enhance students professionalism in the classroom and in the workplace
- To provide an opportunity for leadership development through HOSA and classroom leadership

Course Objectives:
- Students must follow good safety techniques in addition to passing a safety quiz with 100% accuracy.
- Students must follow precisely all written or verbal instructions and procedures given by the instructor.
- Students must be able to perform lab procedures in addition to complete lab write ups, understand the clinical significance of each test performed, and know the normal ranges for each test performed.

Additional Goals For Job Training

Goals	Learning Strategy
Following written instructions	Student must follow written step-by-step instructions for all labs.
Following oral instructions	Students are given additional oral instructions before quizzes, tests, labs, etc., which should be followed exactly to avoid penalties.
Professionalism	Students are taught and graded on professionalism.
Punctuality	Students must be on time for class, or detention will be assigned.
Being charitable	Give charitable gifts during the holiday season.
Proper documentation	Complete daily assignment and daily duties logs.
Accurate documentation	Sign various logs correctly.
Accountability	Stay on tasks and turn in all assignments on time to avoid penalties.

SUPPLIES: *PLEASE GET THESE SUPPLIES AS SOON AS POSSIBLE:*

1. Med lab supplies: TBA
2. 1½ inch black (preferred) three-ring binder with plastic cover
3. Tabs for three-ring binder (See notebook Table of Contents.)
4. Pencil pouch
5. (3) Pens and (3) Number 2 pencils
6. Three (3) red pens, (2) highlighters
7. Paper for note taking
8. Lab coat (Disposal may be provided.)

The class textbooks are:
Clinical Laboratory Science: The Basics and Routine Techniques by Linne and Ringsrud 4th Ed. ISBNL 1-55664-505-8
Medical Parasitology: A Self-Instructional Text by Leventhal and Cheadle 5th Ed. . ISBN: 0-8036-0788-1
If books are lost, the books must be replaced by the student. Books can be purchased at any medical bookstore or online.

LABORATORY NOTEBOOK/STUDENT PORTFOLIO

Students will receive a notebook grade which will count as one major test grade. To receive the maximum points allowed, please set up your laboratory notebook according to your notebook Table of Contents, and review the notebook grade sheet that will be used to grade the notebook. The notebook grade sheet is provided on the back of this sheet.

Principles of Health Science
Grading Policies
Rjackso8@houstonisd.org

I. GRADES
  A. Cheating will not be tolerated, and all penalties will be strictly enforced. See time tracker.
  B. Late work will have a 30-point deduction. A zero will be given after 2 days if work is not submitted.
   a. (Late means that the work was not in student's mailbox station two minutes after teacher calls for assignment or two minutes after student enters the class if late. If student does not have work, student must complete a Late Work Filler Sheet and Excuse Form. Place Filler Sheet in mailbox slot within two minute after teacher calls for assignment. Put the Excuse Forms directly in class color-coded folder, which is located on the teacher's desk. If this process is not completed in the required time, students will lose an additional 10 points off of his or her professionalism grade for not following instructions.
  C. If absent (excused or unexcused) the day of a major exam, students are encouraged to take the exam in class the day the student returns; however, the student will have 3 days to complete the exam. It is the student's responsibility to schedule the makeup exam within the allotted time, or the student will receive a failing grade of zero. It is optional that the teacher make all make-up exams in essay or short answer form. <u>Keep in mind that if a student received a 0 for not making up an exam in the required time, the student can request a retake exam according to school policy.</u>
  D. If a student is absent for any work, it is the student's responsibility to arrange make up within five (5) days. Makeup work can be done by appointment with the teacher before school, during study/tutorial hall, or after school.
  E. A comprehensive final exam will be given at the end of each semester.
  F. Follow school addendum concerning failing major grades and retake policy.
  G. **All test, quizzes, and scantrons are never to leave the classroom. These items are part of official records are kept on file. Review of any test or quiz can be done by appointment either before or after school, during lunch, or during the study hall period.**
  H. All students are different with each student having their own unique way of learning. Therefore, several methods will be used to evaluate a student's performance. Grade breakdown will be as follows:

  50%   Major Grades (tests, major projects, and notebook)
  40%   Daily Grades (quizzes, classwork, etc.)
  10%   Participation (professionalism, homework, and class participation)

II. Tardy Policy (Per Semester)

Being Tardy will not affect numerical grades, however it will affect your conduct grade. *You must be in your assigned seat when the tardy bell rings. If you are not in the classroom when the tardy bell rings, you must obtain a permit from the office in order to enter the classroom.* **TARDY POLICIES WILL BE STRICTLY ENFORCED!!!**

Offense	Consequence (Each tardy, student must sign tardy log)
FIRST Tardy	Warning or other actions by the teacher
SECOND Tardy	½ hour of detention after school (See school policy for days and times.)
THIRD Tardy	1 hour of detention after school and "S" in conduct (See school policy for days and times.)
FOURTH Tardy	2 hours of detention after school (See school policy for days and times.)
FIFTH Tardy	Conduct of "P" in class and student will be placed on probation.
SIXTH Tardy	Student assigned to SAC (off campus). Office conduct of "U"
(or more)	End of the year exit conference with student and parent

III. Conduct (Per Semester)

Conduct is a separate grade. Points will not be taken from your numerical grade for conduct violations; however, bad conduct grades will prevent you from running for elected offices, going on clinical rotations and field trips, receiving scholarships, and **being accepted into AP classes**. Continued conduct violations will result in dismissal from this school. **CONDUCT POLICIES WILL BE STRICTLY ENFORCED!**

CONDUCT OFFENSES

The following is a list of the most common conduct violations that are listed on the conduct log. After **3** conduct violations, the student will receive an **"S"** in conduct. After **4** conduct violations, the student will receive a **"P"** in conduct and be sent to the *office* for discipline. After **5** or more conduct violations, the student will be sent to the office for discipline. Punishment may include parent conference, detention, office "P" or "U", probation, and a review for exit. Students are allowed to serve detention to restore a conduct grade for an "S" to "E" and a "P" to "S" but not a "P" to an "E." See teacher for more details.

Common Violations

a. Failure to be in assigned seat (including leaving class without permission and not signing out to leave)
b. Use of bad language
c. Chewing gum, eating, or drinking in class
d. Applying makeup or combing hair in class
e. Sleeping in class or putting your head down or feet up on desk
f. Talking while test is in progress
g. Writing or passing notes while teacher is lecturing
h. Talking while teacher is lecturing or others are presenting (Raise your hand if you wish to speak.)
i. Horse playing or game playing (cards, listening to personal stereos, calculator games, etc.)
j. Talking too much or too loud
k. Disrespecting instructor or others (This includes taking items off the teacher's desk without permission.)
l. Failure to return required parent signature documents (i.e., policy acknowledgement form, progress reports, etc.).
m. Other offense (See Student Handbook.)

IV. Professionalism Grade

In Introduction to Health Science, you will be receiving a six-week cycle Professionalism Grade that will count as 10% of your total grade. Students are expected to conduct themselves in a professional and courteous manner at all times. In real-life job situations, employees are evaluated on performance and professionalism. Excellent evaluations on a job will usually result in awards and promotions in pay, rank, or both. Poor evaluations may result in either a demotion in pay or rank or being fired.

The rules below must be followed in order to prevent losing points from your Professionalism Grade. You will begin each six weeks with 100 points. Ten (10) points will be taken off each time you violate one of the professionalism rules. Students are allowed to write positive sentences to restore professionalism grades with 3 days of violation. See teacher. Every week, students will receive a Professionalism Grade paycheck.

The Professionalism Grade rules are as follows:

A. Safety Violations

1. Unauthorized or improper handling of instruments or equipment or supplies
2. Failure to wear proper attire on daily basis (i.e., standardize school attire, proper shoes, etc.)
3. Failure to follow safety instructions (i.e., backpacks, purses, or nonessential items off desk, floor, and aisles at ***all times*)**
4. Failure to replace equipment and supplies in their designated areas
5. Failure to clean up immediate surroundings
6. Failure to disinfect all contaminated areas

B. General Violations (Professional Violations continued)

1. Failure to bring books and notebooks to class on a daily basis.\
2. Failure to take required notes
3. Failure to participate in class activities
4. Failure to follow teacher's instructions on assignments (i.e., working on outside assignments, late work procedure)

V. Policy for leaving class:

Students are allowed six emergencies per semester to be excused from class. After the sixth emergency, each time students use a hall pass, it will be considered a tardy.

Notebook Table of Contents for Principles of Health Science
Fall Semester

Binder Cover Sheet (Outside front of notebook/Mission Statement and back of notebook)
Title Page – front/ Notebook Table of Content
Assignment Calendar
Grade Sheet – front/ Notebook Grade Sheets (Cycles 1, 2, and 3)
Orientation Tab/Divider
    Course Syllabus /Overview (front and back copy)
    Grading Policy (front and back copy)
    DeBakey Volunteer Hours Verification Form -front; Guidelines for Community Service Hours -back
    Back to School Bingo -get acquainted activity - front/About Me activity-get acquainted activity-back
    MLA Formant Document (3 pages)
    HOSA Information
Safety Tab/Divider
    Unit 4 Safety Outline
    Unit 4 Safety terms & definitions (handwritten from booklet)
    Safety Learning Activity 1 Questions & Answers - front/Multi-Activity Sheet for Safety - back
    Patient Safety Notes (Unit 2)
    Basic Fire Safety Questions –front / Fire Safety Notes - back
    Fire Safety at Home Learning Activity
    Fire Safety Video Notes (notes written during safety videos)
Communication Tab/Divider
    Communication terms and definitions from all units ((handwritten from booklet)
    Communication Learning Activity 1 Questions & Answers for /Instructions for Notes on Communication Video(s)
    Communication Multi-Information/Activity Sheet
    Chapter 7:3 Human Needs Worksheet
    Communication Video Notes (notes written during communication videos)
Leadership Tab/Divider
    Leadership terms and definitions (handwritten from booklet)
    Leadership Learning Activity 1 Questions & Answers - front /Principles of Leadership notes- back
    Leadership in the World of Word Notes-front/Leadership Multi-Information Sheet - back
    The Criteria for Leadership and History of Medicine Projects
    Leadership Video Notes (notes written during leadership videos)
Parliamentary (Parli.) Procedure Tab/Divider
    National Association of Parliamentarians 300 Study Questions for the NAP Membership Exam
    Using an Agenda – front/How to Election and Officer – back
    Planning a mock meeting – front/Judge Rating Sheet for Mock Meeting – back
    Veritas Model Meeting (front and back)
    Parliamentary Video Notes (notes written during parliamentary videos)
History of Medicine Tab/Divider
    History of Medicine Notes
    History of Medicine Word Search – front/Matching Activity - back
    History of Medicine Video Notes (notes written during history of medicine videos)
Junior Achievement Tab/Divider
    All lessons received from Junior Achievement Volunteer (if applicable)
HOSA Tab/Divider
    All information, event guidelines, and lessons done in class
Final Review Tab/Divider
    Final Review Study Questions (2 pages front and back)
    Final Essay Sheet
Typed homework will not be accepted unless instructed by teacher.

Principles of Health Science
Lesson Plan Assignment Calendar
Cycle 1

Monday	Tuesday	Wednesday	Thursday	Friday
Aug. 27(A/B)	Aug 28(A)	Aug. 29(B)	Aug. 30(A)	Aug. 31(B)
Lesson Plan 1 1st Day of school activities Review course syllabus	Lesson Plan 1 (cont'd.) Orientation Review Grading Policy Watch Video on Dr. DeBakey	Lesson Plan 1 (cont'd.) Orientation Review Grading Policy Watch Video on Dr. DeBakey	Lesson Plan 2 Review Safety Notes Policy Quiz Watch Video on DHSHP	Lesson Plan 2 Review Safety Notes Policy Quiz Watch Video on DHSHP
Sept 3	Sept 4 (A)	Sept 5(B)	Sept 6(A)	Sept 7 (B)
Labor Day	Lesson Plan 3 **Policy Quiz** Write Safety Terms from Booklet Elect Class Officers	Lesson Plan 3 **Policy Quiz** Write Safety Terms from Booklet Elect Class Officers	Lesson Plan 4 **Safety Term Quiz** Do Safety Activity 1 (finish for homework) Elect Class Officers (cont'd.)	Lesson Plan 4 **Safety Term Quiz** Do Safety Activity 1 (finish for homework) Elect Class Officers (cont'd.)
Sept 10 (A)	Sept 11 (B)	Sept 12(A)	Sept 13 (B)	Sept 14 (A)
Lesson Plan 5 Body Mechanics Video **Safety Activity 1 Quiz** Review Unit 2 Notes & Do Multi-activity Sheet (finish for homework) Discuss HOSA EH (Supplies for next class	Lesson Plan 5 Body Mechanics Video **Safety Activity 1 Quiz** Review Unit 2 Notes & Do Multi-activity Sheet (finish for homework) Discuss HOSA EH (Supplies for next class)	Lesson Plan 6 Review Fire Safety Handout & Do Basic Fire Safety Questions Do Extemporaneous Poster Floor Plan Homework	Lesson Plan 6 Review Fire Safety Handout & Do Basic Fire Safety Questions Do Extemporaneous Poster Floor Plan Homework	Lesson Plan 7 **Basic Fire Safety Quiz** Fire Safety Video/ Review for Safety Test (Notes and Terms and activities) Write Communication Terms from Booklet
Sept 17	Sept 18 (B)	Sept 19 (A)	Sept 20(B)	Sept 21(A)
Fall Holiday	Lesson Plan 7 **Basic Fire Safety Quiz** Fire Safety Video/ Review for Safety Test (Notes and Terms and activities) Write Communication Terms from Booklet	Lesson Plan 8 **Safety Test** Review Communication Notes in Booklet Do Activity 1 (Finish or Homework) Discuss HOSA Projects (PS, ES, and RS)	Lesson Plan 8 **Safety Test** Review Communication Notes in Booklet Do Activity 1 (Finish or Homework) Discuss HOSA Projects (PS, ES, and RS)	Lesson Plan 9 **Communication Term Quiz (Unit 4 terms)** Body Language Video Review Communication Notes in Booklet Work on HOSA Projects (PS, ES, and RS) Write Terms for Homework
Sept 24(B)	Sept 25(A)	Sept 26(B)	Sept 27(A)	Sept 28(B)
Lesson Plan 9 **Communication Term Quiz (Unit 4 terms)** Body Language Video Review Communication Notes in Booklet Work on HOSA Projects (PS, ES, and RS) Write Terms for Homework	Lesson Plan 10 Present HOSA Speeches (PS, ES, and RS) Continue writing terms for homework	Lesson Plan 10 Present HOSA Speeches (PS, ES, and RS) Continue writing terms for homework	Lesson Plan 11 Cont'd. Speeches Review Communication Notes & terms in Booklet Continue writing terms Do Chapter 7:3 Activity (Finish for homework)	Lesson Plan 11 Cont'. Speeches Review Communication Notes & terms in Booklet Activity 10-1 (listening skills) or Similar Continue writing terms Do Chapter 7:3 Activity (Finish for homework)
Oct 1 (A)	Oct 2 (B)	Oct 3 (A)	Oct 4 (B)	Oct 5 (A)
Lesson Plan 12 Do Activity 11 Review for Communication Test (Notes and Terms and activities) **<u>Notebook Check</u>**	Lesson Plan 12 Do Activity 11 Review for Communication Test (Notes and Terms and activities) **<u>Notebook Check</u>**	Lesson Plan 13 **Communication Test** Review Leadership Notes: Unit 7/ Leadership Write Terms & Do Activity 1 (Finish for Homework)	Lesson Plan 13 **Communication Test** Review Leadership Notes: Unit 7/ Leadership Write Terms & Do Activity 1 (Finish for Homework)	Lesson Plan 14 Discuss and Watch Leadership Videos of student projects End Cycle 1

Note: This is a tentative schedule. Necessary changes will be made depending upon other school activities, and those changes will be announced in class.

Lesson Plan

Instructor: Freshmen Teachers
Principles of Health Science
Subject: <u>Communication</u>

DeBakey HSHP
Lesson Plan 12
A & B Days

OBJECTIVE THE STUDENT WILL:
- ☐ demonstrate listening skills
- ☐ explain how culture influences behavior.
- ☐ identify culturally acceptable and effective gestures, terms, and behaviors
- ☐ use communication techniques that create a positive exchange of information
- ☐ compare and contrast cultural differences
- ☐ explain how understanding cultural beliefs affect you as a healthcare worker
- ☐ present notebook to teacher
- ☐ review of communication test

PREPARATION

Student Resources: * DeBakey Student Booklet

Instructional Aid: * PowerPoint of directions for Activity 11 - Listening Skills penny game

Materials: N/A

PRESENTATION
* Review for communication test
* Read and discuss notes and activities, and answer any questions concerning test.

APPLICATIONS

Related Activities:
* Do listening Communication/do Activity 11 - Listening Skills penny game.
* Read Units 3 and 4, and write terms from DeBakey Student Booklet.
*Notebook Check

Misc. Activities:
* Highlight and read daily lesson plan calendar.
* Leave area neat and clean.

TEST The communication test will serve as an evaluation of the lesson.